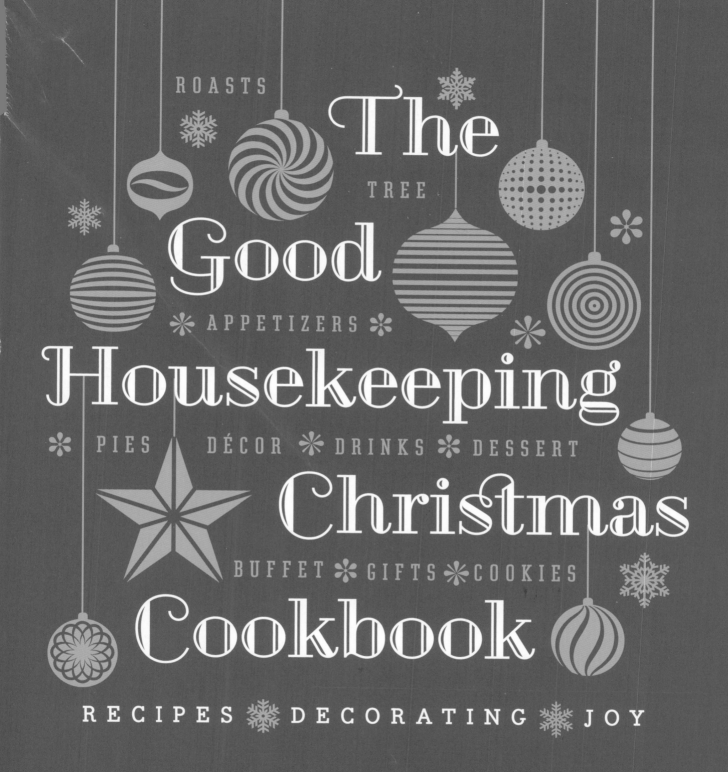

ROASTS

The

TREE

Good

APPETIZERS

Housekeeping

PIES   DÉCOR   DRINKS   DESSERT

Christmas

BUFFET   GIFTS   COOKIES

Cookbook

RECIPES   DECORATING   JOY

HEARST BOOKS
New York

Contents

Chapter 1

Spread the Joy!

THE GREAT CHRISTMAS COUNTDOWN, PREP & CLEANUP

Christmas is the most anticipated of holidays—and with good reason. The season is filled with memorable feasts, an abundance of sweets, decorations that sparkle both indoors and out, and a whirlwind of parties and presents. Most of all, no matter how you and yours celebrate, it's a time to get together—and share the joy—with family and friends.

THE GREAT CHRISTMAS COUNTDOWN

When you were growing up, you may have been asked to help with prep and cleanup, but until you host a holiday meal yourself, you don't truly appreciate the days or even weeks of planning and prep required. To make entertaining easier, we've divided out all the to-do's over eleven days, from planning the menu to serving it. Instead of stressing out with last-minute kitchen chaos, follow this plan and you'll be able to relax and enjoy the party.

But before we launch into the countdown, check your guest list. Invite local friends and family one month before Christmas Day—make that two to three months for out-of-towners, who will need the time to make travel arrangements and hotel reservations. Or, if they're staying with you, you'll want to know ahead of time so you can figure out sleeping arrangements.

December 15th: Check in with Your Guests

If guests haven't confirmed that they're coming, check in with them now. Make sure to ask if they're bringing any children, friends, new significant others, or pets—if furry guests are welcome in your home (if not, make it clear now). For those who can't commit yet, give them until the twentieth to confirm. If they offer to bring food, agree on what dishes they will contribute. If they need suggestions, email them a recipe once you've finalized your menu.

December 16th: Select the Menu

Will it be a formal sit-down dinner with a plated first course, entrée, side dishes, and elegant dessert? Or do you plan to pass platters around the table family style, or let guests serve themselves from a buffet? The serving style you choose will help drive your menu plan. As you select the dishes, keep in mind how much oven, stovetop, and microwave space you have available, and consider what each recipe will require.

Begin by gathering recipes for holiday favorites you like to make every year, then throw some new dishes into the mix. Shop for the ingredients for any new recipes today, and prepare them for your family over the next couple days—they'll let you know if they'd enjoy eating them again. If your guests agreed to bring food, be sure to include these dishes on your menu list. And, if you've invited guests with special dietary needs, work in a selection of dishes they can enjoy. That includes vegetarians, who may be used to feasting on side dishes, but would surely be grateful if you included a meatless main on your holiday menu.

December 17th: Order the Turkey or Roast

Decide which type of turkey (fresh or frozen?), ham (smoked or fresh?), pork roast or beef (tenderloin or standing rib?) to serve and how much to buy (see "How Much Do I Need?" on page 12). If you're ordering a turkey or roast from your butcher, do it today. Ditto if you're ordering a precooked ham online. Place all orders for catered appetizer trays and bakery pies or desserts, too.

December 18th: Take Stock of Your Supplies (and the Guest Room)

Pull out the table linens you plan to use and the hand towels for the bathroom. Are they faded? Have they developed mysterious spots? Wash accordingly. If they're too far gone (or the thought of scrubbing a tablecloth makes you want to weep), snap up some stain-resistant tablecloths and inexpensive hand towels while you're running errands this week.

Pick up some plastic containers; they'll hold prepared items before the meal and leftovers afterward—and make good doggie bags for guests. Also get extra foil and plastic wrap, kitchen twine, trash bags, paper towels, and toilet paper (if you haven't already found this stuff on sale). Consider buying the nonperishable grocery items you need now, too, to shorten the inevitable marathon-shopping trip next week.

Inspect the guest room—by sleeping there. It's the easiest way to find out what's missing (a reading lamp? comfy pillows?). Also, straighten it up now to avoid a mad scramble later. (If guests will sleep on a sofa bed, vacuum the mattress and underneath the cushions.)

December 19th: Grocery Shop, Sharpen Your Knives (and Choose an Outfit!)

Compile a list and shop for all nonperishables, including pantry staples that may be running low. Look for sales in your local circulars and stock up on other holiday musts—paper goods, candies, mixed nuts, beverages, inexpensive toys to entertain kids, batteries for the camera.

Assess your cooking equipment, china, cutlery, and serving dishes. Is the vegetable peeler dull? Are the potholders frayed? Plan to buy or borrow what you'll need. Take inventory of your carving tools. If needed, sharpen them or buy new ones.

Choose your outfit for Christmas Day. It should look good but be comfortable enough for cooking and entertaining. Drop the clothes off at the dry cleaner's if necessary. Nothing to wear? Hit the mall. (If you don't own an apron, pick up one of those, too—prepping a Christmas dinner can get messy.)

CHRISTMAS MENU PLANNING

Holiday meals are a time to think big. A juicy turkey, succulent ham, or standing beef rib roast are all suitably grand centerpieces—the choice often depends on family tradition.

Then make that sideboard groan with accompaniments, from mashed potatoes and stuffings to Brussels sprouts, cranberries—and don't forget the gravy! After dinner, bring on the desserts: cakes, pies, puddings, and cookies. In the chapters that follow, you'll find irresistible recipes for all of these items.

What makes for a winning Christmas menu? Plan for a variety of colors, textures, and flavors. If your main dish is a whole side of salmon, don't start the meal with a seafood pâté. And if you're serving roasted sweet potatoes with your roast beef, add a bit of crunch with broccoli.

The majority of dishes should be those you've cooked and enjoyed in the past. Take advantage of dishes that taste even better made ahead. It's also smart to include some dishes on the menu that freeze well.

Consider how much time you'll need to spend in the kitchen, and incorporate some food prep time-savers accordingly. Avoid including more than two dishes that will require your last-minute attention. Convenience foods like store-bought piecrust; canned or boxed broth; peeled, deveined shrimp; and heat-and-serve ham can all free you up to enjoy the party.

December 20th: Purchase Beverages (and Finalize RSVP's)

Plan what beverages to serve, for both kids and adults. Do you have enough glasses? (If it's a very large group, buy cheap ones in bulk or go for recyclable plastic.) Pick up some drink tags, so guests can easily keep track of their drinks, and coasters if you're concerned about getting rings on your tables.

Wrap up the guest list: You gave any undecided guests a one-week deadline to respond—that's today!

December 21st: Prepare Make-Ahead Dishes (and Select Some Tunes)

Cook the dishes on your menu that will freeze or refrigerate well. Make as many as you can tonight, and plan on preparing the balance over the next two days. Casseroles, soups, cranberry sauce, piecrusts, and cookies are all good candidates for freezing.

Iron linens that need it and lay them out, if you have the space, so they won't rewrinkle.

Create a play list of Christmas favorites for the big day. If your kids are into music, they might enjoy taking on this task. Just be sure to screen their selections to make sure they're holiday appropriate.

December 22nd: Plan the Table Settings (and Polish Your Silver)

Set out your serving dishes and utensils and label them with Post-it notes (e.g., "Brussels sprouts here"). Enlist your partner or kids to make place cards, wash platters, and polish silver, if you're using it. That way, they'll be free to run errands for you and take out the trash the morning of the party. (Once silver is clean, wrap it in tissue, then place in airtight plastic bags to keep it tarnish-free.) Be sure to sharpen your knives— and not just the roast carver. All your kitchen work will go more smoothly.

If you have a frozen turkey or roast, move it from the freezer to the fridge to thaw. Prep any ingredients that will last for two to three days, like chopped onions or fried bacon for the stuffing, and bag them. Continue to make dishes that can be refrigerated or stored until Christmas Day.

December 23rd: Shop for Perishables (and Prepare for Spills)

Shop for all fresh fruits, veggies, and other perishables you'll need to complete your menu. Prepare a make-ahead gravy that will save you time on the big day. Make or buy extra ice.

Thaw frozen make-aheads in the refrigerator, like that piecrust you made two days ago. Prepare the filling and make the pies.

Finally, charge up your hand vac (or just have your broom and dustpan handy)—so you're ready to cope with those unavoidable spills.

December 24th: Cook Some More, Defrost, and Set the Table

Roast or steam the vegetables. Let them cool and then store them in resealable plastic bags in the fridge. Defrost any refrigerated pies or desserts. Decide who will carve the bird or roast. We've gathered all of the help lines you can call in case of a cooking emergency on the big day. Make sure you have easy access to this list.

You've already planned your table; now set it so you don't have to deal with that tomorrow. Place and label trivets with what dish will go where.

Lay out your outfit for the next day, or pick it up from the dry cleaner's if you haven't already.

December 25th: Finish Cooking (and Enjoy the Feast!)

In the morning, get the turkey or other roast into the oven, cook the potatoes (you can keep mashed ones warm in a slow cooker), and make the stuffing and any veggies you haven't prepared yet. Whip the cream for dessert; chill. And don't forget to fill a spray bottle with cold water for zapping stains when they happen.

In the afternoon, add the drippings to the gravy and bring the cranberry sauce to room temperature. If you haven't kept the potatoes warm in a slow cooker, reheat them in the microwave right before serving. Transfer your turkey or roast to a platter. Remove desserts from the refrigerator an hour before serving. Reheat pies in a 350°F oven for 15 minutes and prepare coffee to go with them. If you have the oven space, warm the serving plates there. Otherwise, run them under the hottest water available and quickly dry them just before dinnertime.

Serve, then sit down and enjoy the meal with your guests! You'll of course need to keep an eye out for platters that need replenishing or glasses that need refilling. Ask a close family member or best friend to help with that and assist in clearing the table and serving the dessert and coffee or tea. When the meal is finished, we've heard of a tradition we think all households should institute: Those who cook don't clean up!

MAKE YOUR SILVER FLATWARE SPARKLE

Here are two methods that make polishing silver less of a chore.

The Good Way

Gather a few thick, soft cloths and silver polish. Always follow your product's label directions, but typically, you'll start by putting a dab of polish onto the cloth, dampened if needed.

Rub the polish onto one utensil at a time, going in an up-and-down, not circular, motion to avoid highlighting fine scratches. Work polish into tight areas (between fork tines and into pattern crevices). Turn the cloth frequently as you work, so tarnish isn't deposited back on your silver. Depending on the amount of tarnish, it'll take anywhere from 45 seconds to a few minutes per utensil.

Rinse the cleaned items in warm water; buff to a shine with a clean, dry, soft cloth.

The Good Enough Way

This faster method uses a reaction between aluminum foil and tarnish, where the latter "jumps" from the silver to the foil. Note: Don't use this method for pieces with hollow handles.

Line a plastic (not metal) basin with aluminum foil, shiny side up. Place the silverware inside. Make sure all pieces are contacting the foil or touching a utensil that is.

Sprinkle in ¼ cup washing soda (from grocery or hardware stores). Pour in 1 gallon boiling water. Stir and let the silver soak 10 to 15 minutes.

Wearing rubber gloves, remove the silver. Rinse, and buff with a clean, soft cloth. For very tarnished items, repeat the process.

REMEMBER, IT'S JUST A TURKEY

Some families traditionally serve a pork crown roast, ham, or a prime rib of beef for Christmas dinner, but for many of us, turkey's always the centerpiece of the meal. Whether you're a first-timer or a seasoned holiday cook, our tips will help you prepare and roast the Christmas bird with confidence.

What to Buy

Frozen turkeys are widely available and often on sale during the holidays. Some are prebasted to enhance juiciness. You can buy them well in advance of Christmas, but you'll need to allow enough time for them to thaw before you put them in the oven (see "How to Thaw," below).

Fresh turkeys are preferred by many people but are usually more expensive, have a shorter shelf life, and may need to be special-ordered. Don't buy one more than two days ahead of the big day.

Organic turkeys are raised and fed without the use of antibiotics, hormones, or artificial flavors or colors. It is against the law to use hormones on any turkey, so even frozen nonbranded birds will be hormone free. Free-range turkeys are allowed access to feed outdoors.

Kosher turkeys are available fresh and frozen. They're salted as part of the koshering process, so no additional salt is needed. This process makes the meat tender and juicy, similar to the results you'd get from a brined bird.

How Much to Buy

Estimate 1 pound uncooked turkey per person to ensure enough meat for Christmas dinner and for sandwiches later on. For quantities for stuffing, mashed potatoes, and other essential side dishes, see the chart "How Much Do I Need?" on page 12.

How to Thaw

Remove giblets and reserve for the gravy.

The best way: Place frozen turkey (still in packaging) in a shallow pan on the bottom shelf of the refrigerator. Allow 24 hours thawing time for every 4 to 5 pounds. A thawed bird can keep up to 4 days in the fridge.

Last-minute solution: Place a still-wrapped turkey in a large cooler or bowl and submerge in cold water. Allow 30 minutes of thawing time per pound and change the water every 30 minutes. Cook turkey immediately.

How to Stuff

The best way is to bake stuffing separately in a shallow casserole in the oven alongside the turkey. If you prefer to stuff the bird, follow these guidelines:

Make sure the turkey is fully thawed.

Mix ingredients just before using and stuff loosely into the cavity to allow room for expansion.

Roast the turkey about 30 minutes longer than an unstuffed one.

Check that the internal temperature of the stuffing reaches 165°F.

How to Roast

Place the turkey (breast side up) on a rack in a large roasting pan in an oven preheated to 325°F. If you don't have a rack, place 2 or 3 large carrots crosswise underneath the bird to ensure good heat circulation.

For moist meat, cover with foil from the start—but remove foil during the last hour of roasting for browner, crispier skin.

Basting with pan juices isn't necessary, but it will help with browning after the foil is removed.

Roast turkey 3 to 3¾ hours for a 12- to 14-pounder. (That's around 15 to 17 minutes per pound for an unstuffed bird.)

Use an instant-read meat thermometer to test doneness. Turkey should be taken out of the oven when the thickest part of the thigh (next to but not touching the bone) reaches 175°F and the breast reaches 165°F. Keep in mind that temperature will rise 5°F to 10°F upon standing.

If the turkey is fully cooked earlier than expected, wrap the entire bird and pan with foil and place a large bath towel on top to keep it hot and moist for 1 hour.

Never leave at room temperature longer than 2 hours.

How to Safely Store Turkey Leftovers

The pie has been served, the table is cleared, the dishes await. If you're tempted to curl up in front of a good movie and leave cleanup for the rest of the gang, at least put the turkey away first.

Store it within two hours of serving. Bacteria grow rapidly at room temperature, and refrigeration will not eliminate microorganisms that have already grown," says Sandy Kuzmich, PhD, the GH Institute's Chemistry Director.

Leftover turkey can be refrigerated for 3 to 4 days. In the freezer it will keep for 4 months (plain) or 6 months (in broth or gravy). Here are some additional pointers for safe stowaways:

Take all meat off the carcass and store in serving-size packets or shallow containers. The smaller the portion, the faster you can thoroughly defrost and reheat it. (To refrigerate the packets, wrap meat in plastic wrap or foil and place in self-sealing plastic bags. To freeze, use same procedure but with freezer-weight bags.)

To thaw leftover turkey, place it in the refrigerator overnight. To warm, stir in hot gravy just to heat through. Or stir frozen turkey shreds or small pieces directly into soups at last minute; cook just until hot.

WHEN IN DOUBT

If you're having a turkey meltdown . . .

Try these phone numbers and Web sites for help.

Butterball Turkey-Talk Line
800-288-8372, November 1 to December 29; butterball.com.

USDA Meat and Poultry Hot Line
888-674-6854; www.fsis.usda.gov/education.

Reynolds Turkey Tips Hot Line
800-433-2244, November 1 to December 31; reynoldskitchens.com/holiday-central.asp.

And, if you have any cranberry-related questions, you can get help here.

Ocean Spray's Consumer Affairs Hot Line
800-662-3263; oceanspray.com.

HOW MUCH DO I NEED?

Cooking for a crowd can be daunting— you may know how much stuffing to make for eight people, but how much for twenty? Our at-a-glance guide provides quantities for holiday basics.

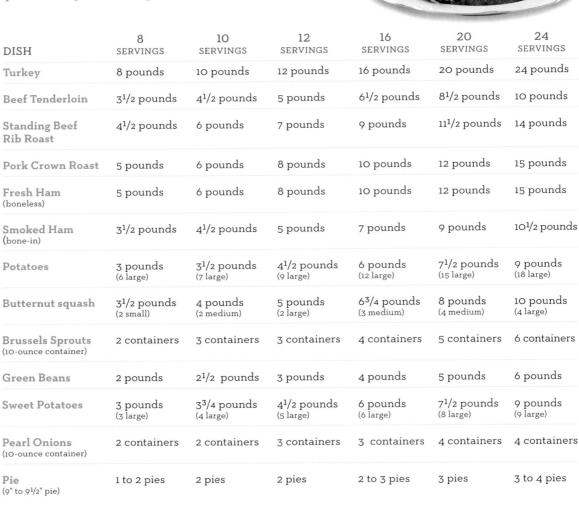

DISH	8 SERVINGS	10 SERVINGS	12 SERVINGS	16 SERVINGS	20 SERVINGS	24 SERVINGS
Turkey	8 pounds	10 pounds	12 pounds	16 pounds	20 pounds	24 pounds
Beef Tenderloin	3¹/2 pounds	4¹/2 pounds	5 pounds	6¹/2 pounds	8¹/2 pounds	10 pounds
Standing Beef Rib Roast	4¹/2 pounds	6 pounds	7 pounds	9 pounds	11¹/2 pounds	14 pounds
Pork Crown Roast	5 pounds	6 pounds	8 pounds	10 pounds	12 pounds	15 pounds
Fresh Ham (boneless)	5 pounds	6 pounds	8 pounds	10 pounds	12 pounds	15 pounds
Smoked Ham (bone-in)	3¹/2 pounds	4¹/2 pounds	5 pounds	7 pounds	9 pounds	10¹/2 pounds
Potatoes	3 pounds (6 large)	3¹/2 pounds (7 large)	4¹/2 pounds (9 large)	6 pounds (12 large)	7¹/2 pounds (15 large)	9 pounds (18 large)
Butternut squash	3¹/2 pounds (2 small)	4 pounds (2 medium)	5 pounds (2 large)	6³/4 pounds (3 medium)	8 pounds (4 medium)	10 pounds (4 large)
Brussels Sprouts (10-ounce container)	2 containers	3 containers	3 containers	4 containers	5 containers	6 containers
Green Beans	2 pounds	2¹/2 pounds	3 pounds	4 pounds	5 pounds	6 pounds
Sweet Potatoes	3 pounds (3 large)	3³/4 pounds (4 large)	4¹/2 pounds (5 large)	6 pounds (6 large)	7¹/2 pounds (8 large)	9 pounds (9 large)
Pearl Onions (10-ounce container)	2 containers	2 containers	3 containers	3 containers	4 containers	4 containers
Pie (9" to 9¹/2" pie)	1 to 2 pies	2 pies	2 pies	2 to 3 pies	3 pies	3 to 4 pies

CHRISTMAS CLEANUP— FROM BEFORE TO BEYOND!

Decorating the house for the holidays is always a pleasure. Cleaning it up before guests arrive and after they leave—not so much. The good news: We've gotten it down to a science. See our tips for fast pre-party fixes and quick cleanup.

Ready, Set Guests!

Company's coming—in twelve minutes. Tackle these hot spots before the doorbell rings: a cluttered entryway, disheveled living room, and not-quite-spotless bathroom.

Overhaul the front hall. Grab a laundry basket, storage bin, or large shopping bag to serve as a junk receptacle, plus a plastic grocery bag and microfiber cloth. Load up your bin with any shoes, gloves, or hats that litter the foyer. Stash hall-table clutter that could get lost (mail, keys) in the plastic bag; put the bag into the bin. While you're near the door, shake doormats outside. Flip on the light for an indoor cobweb check; flick webs off with the cloth (don't worry about ones too high up—chances are, visitors won't notice them once they see your smiling face). Take your bin and keep moving—**3 minutes.**

Put the living room in order. Next stop: where guests will hang out most. Keep filling the bin with kids' toys, newspapers, and anything else that doesn't need to be here. Run your microfiber cloth over the coffee table and other dusty surfaces, like the TV screen. Pile magazines or books into neat stacks on the end tables; gather all of the stray remotes in one place. Plump up throw pillows and chair cushions (even easier: flip the latter, if possible). Use a clean corner of the microfiber cloth to nab any obvious clumps of pet hair or dust stuck to upholstery or carpeting. Drape throws to hide dingy chair arms or furniture stains. Drop off the bin in the laundry room or a nearby bedroom, or hide it in a closet; swap the cloth for a few paper towels. Move on to the bathroom—**4 minutes.**

Fake a super-clean bathroom. Tuck stuff from the vanity into the cabinet or drawers, and close the shower door or stretch out the curtain (sure, nosy guests may still snoop inside, but at least you've cut down on visual clutter). Wet a paper towel with rubbing alcohol to both clean and shine, and wipe down the mirror, faucet, sink, and countertop. Use a new alcohol-dipped towel to go over the toilet seat and rim. Clean up spots and hair from the floor with a third water-dampened paper towel. Finally, put out fresh hand towels. Make a round-trip to the kitchen with the wastebasket to dump it into the larger trash can—**5 minutes.**

MAKE IT EASIER

These organizers and cleaning supplies will make tidying up even quicker.

• **Add a shoe bag** to the inside of your entryway closet door: It makes a great stash spot for hats and gloves, unopened mail, and (yep) shoes when you're picking up in a hurry.

• **Store a pet-hair-removal tool,** in a living room drawer or cabinet, so it's handy.

• **Premoistened disinfecting wipes** like those from Clorox, which are ready for cleaning right out of the canister, will speed up any job.

Crystal-Clear Solutions

Wonder how to make your special glasses and candlesticks sparkle with all the other demands of the holiday season? Here are our fast fixes for spots on stemware, sediment inside narrow-neck vases, and melted wax stuck to candleholders. Before you begin, gather the following tools: white vinegar, a plastic basin, a lint-free towel, baking soda, dish liquid, ammonia, white rice, and a delicate scrub sponge.

Clarify cloudy glasses. Nothing dresses up a holiday dinner table more than beautiful crystal goblets. If yours are looking foggy, hard water is most likely to blame. To remove deposits—no scrubbing required—put 2 cups warm white vinegar (microwave for about two minutes) into a plastic basin. In this, place two glasses, on their sides, for about three minutes, turning to make sure they are bathed in warm vinegar all around. Remove glasses, rinse in clear water, and dry with a lint-free towel. If any spots remain, moisten the glass and sprinkle on some baking soda. With your fingertips, lightly polish it inside and out; rinse and dry.

Deep-clean decanters. When that elegant fluted pitcher or slim vase caught your eye in a store, you probably didn't wonder how you'd clean it. But if liquids or cut flowers have left behind sediment that's impossible to reach, try this: Fill the vessel halfway with very warm water. Squirt in a little dish liquid and add 2 tablespoons ammonia. Pour in about ½ cup white rice and swirl the mixture so the rice "scrubs" the sides of the glass. Let it sit a few minutes to dissolve the residue, and swirl again. Empty, rinse with very warm water, and dry with your lint-free towel. Place the decanter upside down on a rack to allow the interior to drip and air-dry.

Remove wax drips. Candleholders encrusted with melted wax look as if they belong in a thrift shop rather than on your holiday buffet. To quickly remove the clumps from the crevices of cut crystal, fill a basin with hot water and immerse the holders (or place them upside down if the bases are covered with cloth). Let soak several minutes, then peel off the softened wax. If needed, use a delicate scrub sponge or even your fingernail for any stuck-on bits. Wash the wax-free holders in hot, sudsy water; rinse; and dry. Another option, if you have the time: Put caked-up candlesticks in the freezer for two to three hours. The brittle wax will easily chip off; wash and dry.

DECORATING DISASTERS—SOLVED!

Whether the cause is a frisky pet, cavorting kids, or a klutzy moment of your own, sometimes holiday trimmings go down instead of up. Here are some helpful tips to make cleanup less of a chore for when they do.

Broken glass ornaments. Don rubber gloves and gather up the larger chunks of glass into a folded piece of newspaper; tape it closed and place in trash. Skip the fuss of a dustpan and brush; use pieces of soft bread or a dampened paper towel to quickly collect any remaining shards. Vacuum the spot (and a few feet around it, to ensure you've gotten everything; then search for and pick up any fallen ornament hooks before your kids or pets find them.

Spilled glitter. After you've collected mounds of glitter with your vacuum cleaner's hose—no brushes attached—either replace the bag or empty and clean the canister. These tiny particles can get stuck in the filter or clog the bag, reducing suction. Run a lint roller across the floor or carpet to pick up any remaining sparkles. Wipe the bottoms of your shoes (and also your kids') with a damp paper towel to prevent glitter from being tracked around the house.

So Long, Soot!

Old ashes piled up in the firebox? Black soot on the glass, or smoky stains on the surrounding brick, marble, or tile? If your fireplace is sending smoke signals that it needs a scrub, here's the quickest way to get it done—without putting a damper on your day.

Trash the ash. A wet/dry vacuum with a disposable bag will handle the job once the pile has cooled at least four days. But if you don't have one of those heavy-duty suckers, do this instead: After the ash is completely cool, sprinkle it with damp tea leaves or coffee grounds to cover the stale smell and keep down dust (so you won't inhale it). Then scoop the pile with a fireplace shovel (don't worry if you can't get it all—leaving an inch or two behind is fine), and dump it into a metal can or a bucket. Discard the mess outside, ideally in a metal trash container, but definitely away from the house.

Clear things up. To remove light soot or a cloudy film from glass doors, mix a solution of equal parts white vinegar and warm water and pour into a spray bottle. Spritz a bit on a paper towel and dip it into the fireplace ashes to use as a gentle abrasive. To finish, spray glass and wipe clean with a micro-fiber cloth. If soldered-on gunk won't budge (and if you really care), scrape it away with a razor blade.

Brush it off. If you have smoke stains on your fireplace facing, begin by squirting them with water—it'll keep the cleaning solution from soaking in too fast (this is particularly important with brick). Then dip a brush in a solution of ¼ cup all-purpose cleaner to 1 gallon water; give spots a quick scrub; rinse with a clean sponge; let dry. For marble or other stones, squirt with water, then go over the surface with a soft cloth dipped in mild dishwashing liquid and water. Rinse and wipe dry. One exception: If brick facing is more than 50 years old, it may crumble if you scrub with a cleaner. Just vacuum the surface with your soft-brush attachment.

MAKE IT EASIER

Buy the right equipment—or hire a pro to take care of the job.

• **Have tools at the ready.** Buy a dust mask, a metal bucket with a lid to contain ashes, and a commercial cleaner designed to remove soot and smoke stains from brick, stone, and glass (all products are available at local hardware stores or home centers).

• **Hire an expert.** Consider scheduling an appointment for an annual chimney checkup with a professional sweep certified by the Chimney Safety Institute of American (csia.org).

Fast, After-the-Feast Cleanup

Once guests go home, it's just you—and the mess. Here's how to tackle leftovers, from a crumb-covered table to an overflowing trash can and dirty dishes in the sink.

Clear the table. If you only have the energy to get one room in shape tonight, the dining room is the easiest to accomplish. Take any remaining dishes, cups, and serving utensils into the kitchen. Then gather up the tablecloth, and shake crumbs over the kitchen sink or garbage can, or just take a step out your back door and toss the crumbs in the yard or nearest flower bed. Carry all the table linens to the washing machine. Fill it with warm water, add detergent, and leave the items to soak overnight (if you have a spare second, scan the fabrics for stains, sauce, gravy—and pretreat before soaking); you can finish the cycle in the morning.

Deal with leftovers. Food that you would normally refrigerate shouldn't sit out at room temperature for more than a couple of hours. So toss anything that's been out longer. Cover any leftovers you plan to keep with foil or plastic wrap before refrigerating (most baked goods can stay out once covered or wrapped); if needed, transfer food to smaller airtight containers the next day when you have more time.

Take out the trash. If there's room in the kitchen trash can, scrape dishes as well as cooled grease or unwanted gravy from pans into it—it's faster than emptying the sink to get at your garbage disposal, and better for your pipes, too. Seal up the bag; set by the back door. You can haul it to the outdoor garbage can in the morning.

Conquer the counters. Last, tackle what's left in and around the sink. Squirt grimy pots and pans with dishwashing liquid, and fill with very hot water. Set them aside on the counter overnight—this extended soak will make them much easier to hand-wash later. Fill empty space in the dishwasher with dirty plates, glasses, and flatware, but don't bother to prerinse, because the machine will do the work for you (yes, really). Add the detergent and start the cycle. With any remaining dinnerware items, rinse and stack neatly in the sink. They'll get their turn at the dishwasher tomorrow.

MAKE IT EASIER

Just a little bit of preplanning will save you loads of time later.

• **Double- or triple-line the trash can,** so you already have a clean bag in place when a full bag is removed.

• **Have your kids or partner unload the dishwasher** before the guests arrive, so you'll have an empty machine ready to go for the after-dinner cleanup.

• **Line broiling or roasting pans with foil** before using, so baked-on bits, grease, and drippings are easily tossed away.

Christmas Decoration Storage Ideas

The stockings may still be hung by the chimney with care, but Santa's come and gone—and it's time to un-trim the tree before every last needle drops off. So recruit the family, crank up the carols one last time, and make the takedown (and next year's put-up) less painful.

Get packing. Start by packing away decorations in customizable storage that doesn't cost a thing, such as grocery- or liquor-store castoffs. Tape an old holiday card onto each box, so you can easily spot it in the attic or basement, and add a label. That way, you don't have to look through ten boxes just to find the tree topper.

Salvage storage. If your original ornament boxes are dented disasters (or you just forgot to save them), don't worry. Ask your local liquor store for boxes with cardboard dividers, which you can fold and cut as needed. Then layer two to three ornaments wrapped in tissue paper into each slot, placing heavier ones on the bottom. Also, look around the house for storage ideas: egg cartons for tiny trinkets, plastic produce containers or shoeboxes for bigger baubles, paper-towel tubes for garlands.

What if you have an artificial tree but not the box it came in? Stow the faux foliage in an inexpensive, oversize duffel bag to keep the tree clean and its branches from being crushed during the off season.

Handy hanger. Treat wreaths with the same care you give your favorite party dress. Slip the hoop over the neck of a coat hanger, then cover it with a plastic dry cleaning bag to prevent a year's worth of dust from building up. Hang the wreath in a closet or from a beam in your attic.

Bright idea. Wind unwieldy strings of lights around coffee cans, and toss replacement bulbs in the cans. Cut an X in the plastic top, and stick the plug through. Label each string with masking tape and a marker to remind you which lights go on the tree and which wind around doorways.

Keep vs. Toss

• **Keep stockings**—and not the kind that hang from the mantel: Old hosiery can protect specialty candles from getting damaged. Slip knee-highs over the pillars to keep them dust-free. Then, nestle them in tissue paper to prevent dents or scratches, and stow away from heat or pressure, which can melt or warp the wax.

• **Toss newspaper padding.** While it might seem eco-friendly to wrap fragile ornaments in yesterday's news, the ink can smudge decorations. Opt for white tissue paper (colored sheets can bleed) or plastic grocery bags.

• **Keep notes about your decorations:** what worked, where they went, what you need to replace—even Santa makes a list! Stash the info in the box you'll open first.

Festive Beginnings

WELCOMING APPETIZERS, FIRST COURSES, DRINKS & SETTING THE SCENE

Throw open your doors and invite friends and family to indulge in a selection of elegant holiday drinks and delectable hors d'oeuvres. Or choose a festive first-course salad or soup to whet their appetites. Either way, here are tempting recipes to help you set the stage.

Recipes

Crafts

WARM CRAB DIP

Warm Crab Dip

Provide crackers or bread or cucumber rounds and invite your guests to take a dip!

Active time: 10 minutes
Total time: 20 minutes
Makes: 4 cups

1 pound lump crabmeat
1/2 cup butter (1 stick), cut up
2 packages (8 ounces each) Neufchâtel cheese, cut up
1/4 teaspoon cayenne (ground red) pepper
1 green onion, thinly sliced
Toasted bread rounds or crackers for serving

1 Pick through crabmeat to remove any shell or cartilage, making sure not to break up large pieces of meat.

2 In 3-quart saucepan, heat butter, Neufchâtel, and cayenne over medium-low heat about 6 minutes, stirring constantly, until mixture is warm and creamy.

3 Transfer dip to mini slow cooker or fondue pot to keep warm, or transfer to serving bowl. Sprinkle with green onion; serve crab dip with toasted bread or crackers.

Each 2-tablespoon serving: About 80 calories, 4g protein, 0g carbohydrate, 6g total fat (4g saturated), 0g fiber, 34mg cholesterol, 130mg sodium

Savory Blue Cheese, Walnut, and Date Rugelach

Filling rich cream-cheese dough with a mixture of blue cheese, walnuts, and dates turns rugelach into delicious appetizer pastries.

Active time: 40 minutes
Total time: 1 hour 10 minutes plus chilling
Makes: 48 rugelach

1 cup butter or margarine (2 sticks), softened
1 package (8 ounces) cream cheese, softened
2 cups all-purpose flour
1/2 teaspoon salt
1 1/2 cups walnuts
4 ounces blue cheese, cut into small pieces
48 pitted dates (about 12 ounces)
1 large egg white
1 teaspoon water

1 In large bowl, with mixer on medium speed, beat butter and cream cheese until creamy, occasionally scraping bowl with rubber spatula. Reduce speed to low; gradually beat in flour and salt just until blended.

2 Divide dough into 4 equal pieces; shape each into disk. Wrap each disk in plastic wrap and refrigerate until firm enough to roll, at least 4 hours or overnight.

3 In food processor with knife blade attached, process 1/2 cup walnuts until finely chopped; transfer to small bowl. In same bowl, process blue cheese and remaining 1 cup walnuts just until coarse mixture forms.

4 Preheat oven to 350°F. Line two large cookie sheets with foil; grease foil.

5 On lightly floured surface, with floured rolling pin, roll one disk of dough into 10-inch round. (If dough is too cold to roll, let stand 5 to 10 minutes at room temperature to soften slightly.) With pastry wheel or knife, cut dough into 12 equal wedges but do not separate pieces. Beginning 1 inch from edge, sprinkle 1/2 cup blue-cheese mixture in 2-inch-wide ring, leaving dough in center exposed. Place 1 whole date horizontally on wide curved end of each wedge. Separate wedges, and starting at wide end, roll up each wedge, jelly-roll fashion. Place rugelach, point side down, on cookie sheet. Repeat with remaining dough (one disk at a time), blue-cheese mixture, and dates, arranging all rugelach at least 1 inch apart on sheets.

6 In small bowl, lightly beat egg white with water. Brush rugelach with mixture and sprinkle with reserved walnuts.

7 Bake until golden, 30 to 35 minutes, rotating cookie sheets between upper and lower oven racks halfway through. Immediately transfer rugelach to wire racks to cool. Store in airtight container up to 3 days, or in freezer up to 3 months.

Each rugelach: About 125 calories, 2g protein, 10g carbohydrate, 9g total fat (4g saturated), 1g fiber, 18mg cholesterol, 115mg sodium

Prosciutto-Wrapped Breadsticks

These Italian-style breadsticks couldn't be easier—or more delicious! Breadsticks such as Stella d'oro brand are available at grocery stores, or purchase artisanal ones.

Total time 15 minutes • Makes: 30 sticks

30 thick breadsticks
3/4 pound very thinly sliced prosciutto
2/3 cup freshly grated Parmesan cheese

1 Place oven rack 4 inches from broiler heat source. Preheat broiler on High.

2 Wrap each breadstick from top to bottom with prosciutto. Place on cookie sheet. Sprinkle with Parmesan cheese.

3 Broil 30 seconds to 1 minute or until Parmesan has melted.

Each serving: About 70 calories, 5g protein, 7g carbohydrate, 2g total fat (1g saturated), 0g fiber, 10mg cholesterol, 380mg sodium

Cheddar Crab Puffs

These melt-in-your-mouth puffs are sure to be a hit.

Active time: 15 minutes
Total time: 40 minutes
Makes: about 42 puffs

3/4 cup water
4 tablespoons butter or margarine, cut up
1/4 teaspoon salt
1/4 teaspoon ground black pepper
3/4 cup all-purpose flour
3 large eggs
4 ounces extra-sharp Cheddar cheese, shredded (1 cup)
6 ounces lump crabmeat, picked over

1 Preheat oven to 400°F. Line two cookie sheets with parchment paper. Then, in 3-quart saucepan, combine water, butter, salt, and pepper. Heat to boiling on medium. Remove from heat. Add flour and stir until ball forms. Stir in eggs, one at a time, until dough is smooth and shiny. Stir in Cheddar and crab.

2 With tablespoon-size cookie scoop, scoop mixture into balls onto parchment, 1 inch apart. Bake 25 to 30 minutes or until golden brown, rotating sheets between upper and lower racks halfway through. Serve warm. (To make ahead, place in resealable plastic bag; freeze up to 1 month. Reheat frozen puffs in 400°F oven 8 to 10 minutes.)

Each 2-puff serving: About 75 calories, 4g protein, 4g carbohydrate, 5g total fat (2g saturated), 0g fiber, 40mg cholesterol, 125mg sodium

PROSCIUTTO-WRAPPED BREADSTICKS

CHEDDAR CRAB PUFFS

Stuffed Eggs

These make-ahead appetizers are perfect for a crowd. Cook a couple dozen eggs and try all our variations!

Active time: 30 minutes
Total time: 40 minutes plus chilling
Makes: 12 appetizer servings

6 large eggs
1/4 cup mayonnaise
1 tablespoon milk
1/8 teaspoon salt

1 In 3-quart saucepan, place eggs and enough *cold water* to cover by at least 1 inch; heat to boiling over high heat. Immediately remove from heat and cover tightly; let stand 15 minutes. Pour off hot water and run cold water over eggs to cool. Peel eggs.

2 Slice eggs lengthwise in half, cutting around yolks. Gently remove yolks and place in small bowl; with fork, finely mash yolks. Stir in mayonnaise, milk, and salt until evenly blended. Egg-yolk mixture and whites can be covered separately and refrigerated up to 24 hours.

3 Place egg whites in jelly-roll pan lined with paper towels (to prevent eggs from rolling). Spoon egg-yolk mixture into pastry bag fitted with star tip or resealable plastic bag with one corner cut off. Pipe about 1 tablespoon yolk mixture into each egg-white half. (Alternatively, spoon filling into eggs.) If not serving right away, cover eggs and refrigerate up to 4 hours.

Each piece: About 70 calories, 3g protein, 0g carbohydrate, 6g total fat (1g saturated), 0g fiber, 109mg cholesterol, 82mg sodium

Bacon-Horseradish Stuffed Eggs

Prepare yolk mixture as directed, adding **2 tablespoons crumbled crisp-cooked bacon** and **1 tablespoon bottled white horseradish**. If not serving right away, sprinkle crumbled bacon on top of stuffed eggs instead of adding to yolk mixture.

Each piece: About 80 calories, 4g protein, 1g carbohydrate, 7g total fat (2g saturated), 0g fiber, 110mg cholesterol, 102mg sodium

Dried Tomato–Caper Stuffed Eggs

Prepare yolk mixture as directed, adding **5 teaspoons chopped dried tomatoes packed in oil and herbs, 5 teaspoons chopped drained capers,** and **1/8 teaspoon coarsely ground black pepper.**

Each piece: About 80 calories, 3g protein, 1g carbohydrate, 7g total fat (1g saturated), 0g fiber, 109mg cholesterol, 143mg sodium

Lemon-Basil Stuffed Eggs

Prepare yolk mixture as directed, adding **1 tablespoon chopped fresh basil, 1/4 teaspoon freshly grated lemon peel,** and **1/4 teaspoon coarsely ground black pepper.**

Each piece: About 75 calories, 3g protein, 0g carbohydrate, 6g total fat (1g saturated), 0g fiber, 109mg cholesterol, 82mg sodium

Pimiento-Studded Stuffed Eggs

Prepare yolk mixture as directed, adding **2 tablespoons chopped pimientos, 2 teaspoons Dijon mustard,** and **1/8 teaspoon cayenne (ground red) pepper.**

Each piece: About 75 calories, 3g protein, 1g carbohydrate, 6g total fat (1g saturated), 0g fiber, 109mg cholesterol, 102mg sodium

Mini Rémoulade Crab Cakes

Crab cakes are a universal favorite, and they are especially good paired with our lemon-mayo sauce. These luscious morsels can be prepared up to several hours ahead and refrigerated. Reheat the crab cakes and prepare the sauce just before serving.

Active time: 25 minutes
Total time: 45 minutes plus chilling
Makes: 50 mini crab cakes

Crab Cakes

2 tablespoons butter or margarine
1 small onion, finely chopped
1/2 red pepper, finely chopped
1 stalk celery, finely chopped
1/4 cup light mayonnaise
1 tablespoon sour cream
2 teaspoons grainy Dijon mustard
1/2 teaspoon freshly grated lemon peel
1/4 teaspoon salt
1/8 teaspoon cayenne (ground red) pepper
1 pound lump crabmeat, picked over
1 cup fresh bread crumbs (about 2 slices bread)

Lemon Sauce

1/4 cup light mayonnaise
1/4 cup sour cream
1 teaspoon freshly grated lemon peel
1 tablespoon fresh lemon juice
Pinch salt
Pinch cayenne (ground red) pepper

1 In 10-inch skillet, melt butter over medium heat. Add onion, red pepper, and celery. Cook, stirring frequently, until vegetables are tender, about 10 minutes. Let cool.

2 In large bowl, stir mayonnaise, sour cream, mustard, lemon peel, salt, and cayenne until blended; stir in crabmeat and bread crumbs just until mixed. Cover and refrigerate 30 minutes.

3 Meanwhile, prepare lemon sauce: In small bowl, combine mayonnaise, sour cream, lemon peel and juice, salt, and cayenne, stirring until blended. Makes 1/2 cup.

4 Preheat oven to 400°F. Lightly grease two cookie sheets. Drop level tablespoons crabmeat mixture onto prepared cookie sheets and press lightly to form patties. Bake until golden brown, about 15 minutes. Top each crab cake with about 1/2 teaspoon lemon sauce. Serve hot.

Each crab cake with sauce: About 30 calories, 2g protein, 1g carbohydrate, 2g total fat (1g saturated), 0g fiber, 12mg cholesterol, 71mg sodium

Holiday Spritzers

Enjoy this refreshing drink.

Total time: 10 minutes plus chilling
Makes: 8 servings

1 can (8 ounces) frozen limeade concentrate, thawed
2 cups water
3 cups tart cherry, pomegranate, or cranberry juice
2 limes
2 cups lemon-lime seltzer, or more to taste
Ice cubes for serving

1 In pitcher, combine undiluted limeade concentrate and water until well blended. Stir in juice. Slice each lime crosswise into ¼-inch-thick wheels; cut a slit in each wheel, from center to edge.

2 To serve, place ice cubes in each glass; pour in about ¾ cup juice mixture and top with about ¼ cup seltzer. Place a lime wheel on the rim of each glass. Or, pour mixture into punch bowl and add 2 cups seltzer, or more to taste. Add ice cubes or ice mold.

Each serving: About 140 calories, 0g protein, 36g carbohydrate, 0g total fat, 0g fiber, 0mg cholesterol, 8mg sodium

Warm Spiced Cider

This holiday favorite is spiced with cinnamon, cloves, and citrus.

Active time: 10 minutes
Total time: 30 minutes
Makes: 16 cups or 16 servings

1 large orange
12 whole cloves
Peel from 1 lemon, removed in continuous 1-inch-wide strip
6 cinnamon sticks (3 inches each)
1 gallon apple cider

1 Cut two ½-inch-thick slices from center of orange. Stick cloves into skin around each orange slice. Cut remaining orange into thin slices for garnish.

2 In nonreactive 5-quart saucepot over high heat, heat orange slices with cloves, lemon peel, cinnamon sticks, and apple cider to boiling. Reduce heat to low; cover and simmer 15 minutes.

3 Pour hot cider through strainer into large (5-quart) heat-safe punch bowl. Place remaining orange slices in cider for garnish. Serve immediately.

Each serving: About 105 calories, 0g protein, 28g carbohydrate, 0g total fat, 0g fiber, 0mg cholesterol, 5mg sodium

Hot Chocolate

On a wintery day, hot chocolate topped with a dollop of whipped cream is comfort-in-a-cup. For the ultimate indulgence, serve with our festive DIY Hot Cocoa Dippers, at right.

Total time: 10 minutes
Makes: 4 cups or 12 servings

1 cup heavy cream
2 tablespoons confectioners' sugar
2 teaspoons vanilla extract
6 ounces semisweet chocolate, chopped
1⅔ cups boiling water
1½ cups whole milk
Unsweetened cocoa for sprinkling (optional)

1 In small bowl, with mixer on medium speed, beat cream with sugar and vanilla until stiff peaks form. Cover and refrigerate if not using whipped cream right away.

2 Place chocolate in 1-quart saucepan. Pour ⅓ cup boiling water over chocolate and stir until chocolate melts. Whisk in milk and remaining 1⅓ cups boiling water; cook over medium heat until hot but not boiling, whisking constantly.

3 Ladle hot chocolate into mugs and dollop with whipped cream. Sprinkle with cocoa, if you like, and serve.

Each serving: About 165 calories, 2g protein, 11g carbohydrate, 13g total fat (8g saturated), 1g fiber, 32mg cholesterol, 25mg sodium

Hot Cranberry-Cider Punch

Serve this warming blend of apple cider, cranberry-raspberry juice, and spices at an open house.

Active time: 10 minutes
Total time: 30 minutes
Makes: 16 cups or 16 servings

2 teaspoons whole cloves
2 teaspoons whole allspice
5 small oranges
½ gallon apple cider or apple juice
2 cans (12 ounces each) frozen cranberry-raspberry
   juice concentrate
4 cinnamon sticks (3 inches each)
½ cup packed brown sugar
8 cups water
1 small lemon, whole cloves, and cranberries for garnish

1 Wrap cloves and allspice in piece of double-thickness cheesecloth to make a spice bag; tie with string. From 4 oranges, squeeze juice; reserve 1 orange for garnish.

2 In 6-quart saucepot over high heat, heat spice bag, orange juice, apple cider, undiluted cranberry-raspberry juice concentrate, cinnamon sticks, brown sugar, and water to boiling. Reduce heat to low; cover and simmer 20 minutes. Discard spice bag.

3 Meanwhile, prepare garnish: Cut reserved orange into slices. Thinly slice lemon. Arrange lemon slices on top of orange slices, securing with cloves and garnishing with cranberries.

4 To serve, pour hot punch into large (5-quart) heat-safe punch bowl. Gently place citrus slices in punch.

Each serving: 85 calories, 1g protein, 26g carbohydrate, 0g total fat, 0g fiber, 0mg cholesterol, 5mg sodium

HOT CHOCOLATE

DIY HOT COCOA DIPPERS

Stir up something special this season with our hot cocoa dippers.

Gather large marshmallows, drinking straws, chocolate, and red nonpareil sprinkles. Skewer marshmallows on straws, then melt chocolate in a small vessel (such as a small, microwave-safe bowl). Dip marshmallows in chocolate, leaving white tops exposed; lift sticks straight up, letting excess chocolate drip off. Cool briefly on waxed paper, but dip marshmallow bottoms into sprinkles while chocolate is still slightly soft.

HEALTHY HOLIDAY MAKEOVER: EGGNOG

Traditional eggnog is high in fat, but only a Scrooge would give it up altogether. Our slimmed-down nog contains one-fourth the saturated fat and approximately half the cholesterol while retaining silky texture and decadent flavor. For some people, the classic version is a once-a-year indulgence. We've included both recipes so you can enjoy this holiday staple your way.

Classic Eggnog

Active time: 10 minutes
Total time: 35 minutes plus chilling
Makes: 16 cups or 32 servings

12 large eggs
1¼ cups sugar
½ teaspoon salt
2 quarts whole milk
2 tablespoons vanilla extract
1 teaspoon ground nutmeg plus additional for
   sprinkling
1 cup heavy cream

1 In 5-quart Dutch oven, with wire whisk, beat eggs, sugar, and salt until blended. Gradually stir in 1 quart milk and cook over low heat, stirring constantly, until custard thickens and coats back of spoon well, about 25 minutes. Do not allow mixture to boil, or it will curdle. (Mixture should remain at about 160°F.)

2 Pour custard into large bowl; stir in vanilla, 1 teaspoon ground nutmeg, and remaining 1 quart milk. Cover and refrigerate until well chilled, at least 3 hours.

3 In small bowl, with mixer on medium speed, beat cream until soft peaks form. With wire whisk, gently fold whipped cream into custard mixture.

4 To serve, pour eggnog into chilled 5-quart punch bowl; sprinkle with nutmeg for garnish.

 Each serving. 5g protein, 11g carbohydrate, 7g total fat (4g saturated), 0g fiber, 98mg cholesterol, 90mg sodium

Healthy Makeover Eggnog

Active time: 5 minutes
Total time: 15 minutes plus chilling
Makes: 13 cups or 26 servings

6 large eggs
6 large egg whites
11 cups low-fat milk (1%)
1 cup sugar
¼ cup cornstarch
½ teaspoon salt
¼ cup vanilla
1 teaspoon ground nutmeg plus
   additional for sprinkling

1 In bowl, with whisk, beat eggs and egg whites until blended; set aside. In 5-quart Dutch oven, with heat-safe spatula, mix 8 cups milk with sugar, cornstarch, and salt. Cook on medium-high until mixture boils and thickens slightly, stirring constantly. Boil 1 minute. Remove pot from heat.

2 Gradually whisk 1 cup simmering milk mixture into eggs; pour egg mixture back into milk in saucepan, whisking constantly, to make custard.

3 Pour custard into 5-quart punch bowl; stir in vanilla, nutmeg, and remaining 3 cups milk. Cover and refrigerate until well chilled, at least 6 hours or up to 2 days. Sprinkle eggnog with nutmeg to serve.

Each serving. 6g protein, 14g carbohydrate, 2g total fat (1g saturated), 0g fiber, 53mg cholesterol, 125mg sodium

Spinach and Mandarin Orange Salad

By using prewashed spinach, canned Mandarin orange segments, and bottled dressing, we've created a festive five-minute salad.

Total time: 5 minutes
Makes: 8 first-course servings

2 bags (5 to 6 ounces each) baby spinach
1/3 cup bottled poppy seed salad dressing
1/2 lemon
1 can (11 ounces) Mandarin orange sections, drained
1/2 cup honey-roasted sliced almonds

Place spinach in large salad bowl. Drizzle dressing on top; squeeze juice from lemon half over salad. Just before serving, toss to combine and top with orange sections and almonds.

Each serving: About 95 calories, 3g protein, 6g carbohydrate, 7g total fat (1g saturated), 5g fiber, 0mg cholesterol, 125mg sodium

Cucumber Pomegranate Salad

Sweet-tart pomegranate seeds and apples balance the light licorice flavor of fennel in this crunchy special-occasion salad.

Total time: 30 minutes
Makes: 12 side-dish servings

1 lemon
1/3 cup extra-virgin olive oil
3 tablespoons champagne vinegar
1/2 teaspoon salt
1/2 teaspoon ground black pepper
1 1/2 pounds fennel bulbs
1 seedless (English) cucumber
1 Granny Smith apple, halved, cored, and very thinly sliced
1/2 cup fresh pomegranate seeds

1 From lemon, grate ½ teaspoon peel and squeeze 2 tablespoons juice. In jar or container with tight-fitting lid, combine oil, vinegar, lemon peel and juice, ¼ teaspoon salt, and pepper. Shake well. Dressing can be refrigerated up to 2 days.

2 Pluck 2 tablespoons fennel fronds from fennel tops and reserve for garnish (see Tip). Trim and core fennel. With adjustable-blade slicer or very sharp knife, very thinly slice fennel. With vegetable peeler, peel alternating strips from cucumber skin, then thinly slice cucumber crosswise at angle.

3 On large serving platter, layer fennel, cucumber, and apple. Shake dressing again and drizzle all over. Top salad with pomegranate seeds and fennel fronds. Sprinkle with remaining ¼ teaspoon salt.

TIP: If you buy fennel bulbs without their tops, you can use 2 tablespoons fresh dill for garnish instead.

Each serving: About 85 calories, 1g protein, 8g carbohydrate, 6g total fat (1g saturated), 2g fiber, 0mg cholesterol, 120mg sodium

CUCUMBER POMEGRANATE SALAD

Orange-Endive Ambrosia

For a truly authentic ambrosia, don't skimp on the coconut! It is an essential ingredient for this old-fashioned salad.

Active time: 15 minutes
Total time: 20 minutes
Makes: 8 side-dish servings

½ cup unsweetened coconut flakes
¼ cup low-fat buttermilk
1 tablespoon sherry vinegar
1 teaspoon Dijon mustard
1 tablespoon extra-virgin olive oil
¼ teaspoon salt
¼ teaspoon ground black pepper
4 navel oranges
4 heads Belgian endive
½ cup packed fresh flat-leaf parsley leaves

1 In 12-inch skillet, toast coconut on medium 2 to 4 minutes or until golden, stirring occasionally. Remove from heat and cool completely. (Coconut can be kept at room temperature in airtight container up to 1 day.)

2 In small bowl, with fork, whisk buttermilk with vinegar, mustard, oil, salt, and pepper until well mixed. (Dressing can be covered and refrigerated up to 1 day.)

3 With knife, cut peel and white pith from oranges and discard. Cut each orange crosswise into ¼-inch rounds; cut each round in half and transfer to bowl, keeping some rounds whole if you like. (Oranges can be covered and refrigerated up to 1 day.)

4 When ready to serve, trim endive. Cut crosswise at angle into 1-inch pieces; discard core. In large bowl, toss endive and parsley with dressing until coated.

5 On large serving platter, spread half of oranges decoratively in single layer. Top with endive salad and remaining oranges. Sprinkle with toasted coconut.

Each serving: About 100 calories, 2g protein, 12g carbohydrate, 6g total fat (4g saturated), 3g fiber, 0mg cholesterol, 100mg sodium

ORANGE-ENDIVE AMBROSIA

Roasted-Beet and Pistachio Salad

Delight your guests with this simple but flavorful salad. Roasting the beets enhances their natural sweetness.

Active time: 20 minutes
Total time: 1 hour 20 minutes plus cooling
Makes: 12 side-dish servings

6 beets (4 ounces each; see Tip)
1/2 cup shelled unsalted pistachios
3 tablespoons balsamic vinegar
2 teaspoons Dijon mustard
1/4 teaspoon salt
1/4 teaspoon ground black pepper
1/3 cup extra-virgin olive oil
3 bags (4 ounces each) baby greens and herbs mix
1/4 cup crumbled blue cheese
1/4 cup packed fresh mint leaves

1 Preheat oven to 400°F. Arrange beets in single layer on large sheet of foil and wrap tightly. Place in shallow glass or ceramic baking dish and bake 1 hour or until tender when pierced with tip of knife.

2 While beets bake, place pistachios in small baking pan; place in oven alongside beets until golden and toasted, about 4 minutes. Cool completely in pan.

3 When beets are done, unwrap foil and let beets sit until cool enough to handle. Peel beets and cut into 1/2-inch chunks.

4 Prepare dressing: In small bowl, with fork or wire whisk, mix vinegar, mustard, salt, and pepper until blended. In thin, steady stream, whisk in oil until blended.

5 In medium bowl, combine beets and 2 tablespoons dressing. In large serving bowl, toss greens with remaining dressing until coated. Top with blue cheese, pistachios, and beets. Tear mint leaves over salad.

TIP: No time to roast beets? Swap in packaged cooked beets.

Each serving: About 115 calories, 3g protein, 6g carbohydrate, 9g total fat (2g saturated), 2g fiber, 2mg cholesterol, 120mg sodium

ROASTED-BEET AND PISTACHIO SALAD

Chestnut Parsnip Soup

Puree prepackaged chestnuts with potato and parsnips to create a silky, satisfying soup. See "Roasting Chestnuts," below, if you want to roast your own.

Active time: 30 minutes
Total time: 40 minutes
Makes: 12 appetizer servings

1 jar (14 ounces) peeled, roasted chestnuts
1 tablespoon plus 1 teaspoon butter or margarine
2 pounds parsnips, peeled and chopped (see Tip)
1 large onion (12 ounces), finely chopped
1 all-purpose potato, peeled and chopped
3 cups reduced-sodium chicken broth
4 cups water plus more if needed
2 tablespoons honey
1/2 teaspoon salt
1/4 teaspoon ground black pepper
1/4 cup reduced-fat sour cream
Snipped chives for garnish

1 Cut 12 whole chestnuts in half and reserve. Chop remaining chestnuts.

2 In 6- to 7-quart saucepot, melt 1 tablespoon butter on medium-high heat. Add parsnips, onion, potato, and chopped chestnuts. Cook 2 to 3 minutes or until golden, stirring. Add chicken broth and water. Heat to boiling. Reduce heat to low; cover and simmer 20 minutes or until vegetables are tender.

3 Meanwhile, in 1- to 2-quart saucepan, combine honey and remaining 1 teaspoon butter. Cook on medium heat until bubbling. Add chestnut halves and cook 5 to 7 minutes or until glazed, gently turning occasionally to evenly coat.

4 Working in batches, carefully ladle parsnip mixture into blender. Cover, with center part of lid removed to allow steam to escape (drape with clean kitchen towel to avoid splatter), and blend until smooth. (Blended soup can be covered and refrigerated up to 1 day.) Return soup to saucepot and reheat on medium-low until hot, adding additional water if thinner soup is preferred. Stir in salt and pepper.

5 Divide soup among serving bowls. Swirl 1 teaspoon sour cream into each portion. Garnish with glazed chestnut halves and snipped chives.

TIP: If the cores of the parsnips are tough and woody, cut out and discard them.

Each serving: About 180 calories, 3g protein, 37g carbohydrate, 3g total fat (1g saturated), 5g fiber, 3mg cholesterol, 235mg sodium

ROASTING CHESTNUTS

Chestnuts can be presented in many guises: tossed into almost any stuffing, added to a vegetable medley, or pureed with sugar and vanilla and served with whipped cream.

Step 1: Preheat oven to 400°F. With sharp knife, cut an X in flat side of shell of each chestnut. Place in jelly-roll pan and roast until shells open, about 20 minutes.

Step 2: Cover chestnuts with clean kitchen towel. When cool enough to handle, with paring knife, peel chestnuts, keeping unpeeled ones warm as you work for easier peeling.

Chestnut Parsnip Soup

Lobster Bisque

When you serve lobster, save the shells and cooking liquid and make this splendid soup the next day.

Active time: 15 minutes
Total time: 1 hour 15 minutes
Makes: 4 first-course servings

2 tablespoons butter or margarine
1 onion, chopped
1 carrot, peeled and chopped
1 stalk celery, chopped
1 garlic clove, finely chopped
3 tablespoons tomato paste
Leftover shells and heads from 4 steamed lobsters
2 tablespoons cognac or brandy
6 cups water
2 bottles (8 ounces each) clam juice or
   2 cups cooking liquid from steamed lobsters
3 sprigs parsley
1/8 teaspoon dried thyme
Pinch ground nutmeg
Pinch cayenne (ground red) pepper
3 tablespoons all-purpose flour
3/4 cup heavy cream

1 In 12-quart nonreactive stockpot, melt butter over medium heat. Add onion, carrot, celery, and garlic and cook until onion is tender, about 5 minutes. Stir in tomato paste.

2 Increase heat to high and add lobster shells; cook, stirring occasionally, 5 minutes. Stir in cognac and cook until liquid has evaporated. Add water, clam juice, parsley, thyme, nutmeg, and cayenne; heat to boiling. Reduce heat; cover and simmer 30 minutes.

3 Strain soup through sieve into 4-quart saucepan; discard solids. Heat to boiling over high heat; boil until reduced to 5 cups, 10 to 15 minutes.

4 In small bowl, with wire whisk, whisk flour into cream until blended and smooth. Gradually whisk cream mixture into soup; heat just to boiling, whisking constantly. Reduce heat and simmer 2 minutes.

Each serving: About 260 calories, 3g protein, 12g carbohydrate, 22g total fat (14g saturated), 0g fiber, 77mg cholesterol, 441mg sodium

GARNISHING SOUP

As delicious as soup is unadorned, almost any bowl will be enhanced by a garnish that adds a splash of color and extra flavor.

Chopped fresh herbs are the simplest of garnishes. Choose an herb that complements the soup's flavor and color. For best results, chop or snip fresh herbs just before using. Pureed soups can accommodate more elaborate garnishes. Their smooth texture calls out for a sprinkling of grated cheese, crumbled bacon, or toasted bread or chopped nuts. Pureed vegetable soups are often topped with a drizzle of heavy cream or infused olive oil.

Spiced Pumpkin Soup

Better grab the big bowls—this lush, velvety blend of pumpkin and fall spices will have guests wanting more. To double the yield, see Tip.

Active time: 25 minutes
Total time: 50 minutes
Makes: 6 appetizer servings

2 tablespoons olive oil
1 large onion (8 to 10 ounces), chopped
1 Granny Smith apple, peeled, cored, and chopped
1 carrot, chopped
5/8 teaspoon salt
1/2 teaspoon ground ginger
1/4 teaspoon ground cumin
1/4 teaspoon ground coriander
1 quart chicken broth
3/4 cup light coconut milk
1 can (15 ounces) pureed pumpkin
3 thick slices white bread, crusts removed, cut into
   1/2-inch cubes (3 cups)
3 tablespoons butter (no substitutions), cut up
Pinch cayenne (ground red) pepper
2 tablespoons sour cream

1 Preheat oven to 400°F.

2 In 5-quart saucepot, heat oil on medium heat. Add onion, apple, carrot, and 1/2 teaspoon salt. Cook 10 to 15 minutes or until vegetables are just tender, stirring frequently. Stir in ginger, cumin, and coriander; cook 1 minute.

3 Whisk broth, coconut milk, and pumpkin into pot. Heat to simmering on high. Reduce heat; simmer soup 20 minutes or until slightly reduced, stirring often.

4 Meanwhile, arrange bread cubes on 18" by 12" jelly-roll pan. Bake 7 to 8 minutes or until crisp and golden, stirring once. Cool; transfer to medium bowl.

5 In 10-inch skillet, heat butter on medium 3 to 5 minutes or until golden brown and fragrant, swirling pan. Drizzle butter over bread in bowl; toss to coat.

SPICED PUMPKIN SOUP

(Cooled croutons can be stored in resealable bag up to 4 days at room temperature.)

6 To pot with soup, add cayenne and remaining 1/8 teaspoon salt. Working in batches, blend soup until smooth. Return to pot; heat on medium-low until hot. Serve with croutons and small dollop of sour cream.

TIP: To make 12 servings, in step 2, use 8-quart saucepot, 2 tablespoons olive oil, 2 medium onions (1 pound), 2 apples, 2 carrots, 3/4 teaspoon salt, 1 teaspoon ginger, 1/2 teaspoon cumin, and 1/2 teaspoon coriander. In step 3, use 1 1/2 quarts broth, 1 can (15 ounces) coconut milk, and 1 can (29 ounces) pumpkin. In step 4, use 5 slices bread (5 cups cubes). In step 5, use 5 tablespoons butter. In step 6, use 1/8 teaspoon cayenne, 1/4 teaspoon salt, and 3 tablespoons sour cream.

Each serving: About 250 calories, 4g protein, 26g carbohydrate, 15g total fat (6g saturated), 4g fiber, 17mg cholesterol, 750mg sodium

EASY-TO-MAKE WREATHS TO WELCOME YOUR GUESTS

Ring in glad tidings with creative holiday hoops that are as simple to make as they are sensational. Some use evergreen or winterberry branches you can buy at a florist, while others make use of recycled materials you can find around the house.

1. Winter Wonderland Wreath

Matte white spray paint transforms au naturel grapevine, twigs, and pinecones into an icy-looking Arctic circle. At your craft or floral supply store, purchase an 18-inch grapevine wreath. At the floral supply area of the craft store, look for natural pods in a variety of shapes, pinecones, and seasonal nuts from an assorted-mix package (or forage these items from the outdoors) to add texture and variety to the wreath. Using a hot glue gun, add these dried decorations to the wreath. To make stick stars, use sticks from outdoors broken into 3- to 4-inch lengths or use cinnamon sticks. Glue them on top of each other to form the star shape and add them to the wreath.

When all the pieces have been added, place the wreath on newspaper or another surface you don't mind getting messy, and spray-paint the entire wreath white. Allow to dry. Loop with wire in back to hang.

2. Take It from Him Wreath

Turn Dad's old ties into door décor. You'll need a 14-inch wire wreath and 19 neckties. Cut all the ties but one into 15-inch lengths. Position the narrow end of the first cut tie, front side up, on a section of the wreath. Wrap the tie around the form until the pointed end is positioned as shown; hiding the rolled tie, secure with pins. Repeat, overlapping the ties slightly, until the wreath is covered. Flip the wreath over, sew rolled-up ties to the backs of points. Create a bow from the uncut tie and pin it onto the wreath.

3. Mixed Greens Wreath

This woodsy design, studded with fruit and plants, blends faux and real. From the craft store, purchase a 16-inch grapevine wreath and artificial Granny Smith apples. Use a hot glue gun to affix the apples, spacing them evenly around the ring. Select an assortment of seasonal flora from the florist or the forest—pinecones, fragrant eucalyptus, and juniper—and weave them into the grapevine, filling in the areas between the apples.

TIP: To hang heavier wreaths, you can use a simple nail; paint it to match the door so you can leave it up year-round. For lighter wreaths, use a stick-on hook from 3M, which won't damage the wall.

4. Kumquat and Cranberry Garland Wreath

Kumquats and cranberries stuck into a juniper-covered wreath create a festive garland effect. Wrap a wire around a 16-inch straw wreath to create a hanger. Working diagonally around the wreath, pin rows of kumquats into the wreath with straight pins (available at fabric stores). To each side of the kumquats, add a row of cranberries (also using straight pins). Use florists' pins to attach a wide row of blue juniper in between the rows of fruit. Finish by wiring a red ribbon on top.

5. Candy Cane Door Decor

Who said wreaths had to be hoops? Here, everyone's favorite Christmas confection provides a cheery welcome. Draw a candy cane shape onto a large piece of paper. Cut it out and trace the shape onto a 2-inch-thick piece of Styrofoam. Cut out the Styrofoam shape using a serrated knife. Wrap a piece of white felt 4 inches wider than the candy cane around the shape (use straight pins to attach it to the back). Tightly wrap a wire around the top of your candy cane and create a loop for a hanger on the back. Spread out an assortment of peppermint candies and broken candy canes on a newspaper in a well-ventilated area, like a garage. Spray the pieces with polyurethane, making sure to coat all sides of the candy well; let dry. Use a glue gun to apply the candy to the front and sides of the wreath, then give the whole thing two more coats of polyurethane. Finish by wiring on sprigs of pine and a bow.

BRIGHTEN THE NIGHT WITH FESTIVE OUTDOOR LIGHTS

Come holiday season, even normally unfazed folks feel peer pressure from the neighbors to mount a high-wattage nighttime extravaganza. But struggling with too-short extension cords, snarled strands of bulbs, and the steep utility bill afterward could bring out even Kriss Kringle's dark side.

This year, switch to simple illuminated decorations that will welcome guests to your home with old-fashioned charm. The understated displays shown here are as inexpensive as they are easy. All you need are candles, battery-powered fairy lights, and household items like canning jars. And since there are no teetering ladders involved, even the tiniest tots can help get things glowing. If you use lighted candles, just be sure never to leave them unattended.

1. Yuletide Yard Tree

Give an evergreen tree the star treatment by encircling it with twinkling candlelight: Spray-paint metal buckets a jolly yuletide red, then pack them to overflowing with snow (or sand if the weather is balmy). Insert tapers, and surround with clear glass hurricanes to shield flames from the elements. Santa hat on the tree is optional (though definitely fun!).

2. Snow Motion

Guests get an anything-but-chilly reception with this sports-inspired entryway. Search eBay and flea markets for vintage winter gear, like Flexible Flyers, ice skates, and wooden skis (or you may already have these items stashed in your garage or attic!). Attach skates to a wreath hanger, lean heavier items, like the metal-runner sleds, nearby, and accessorize with prelit artificial wreaths.

3. Window Dressing

Sprucing up a winter-weary window planter couldn't be simpler: Position a pair of pagoda-shaped lanterns in the box (use battery operated candles for safety), then tuck in greenery all round them. To add a splash of holiday color, you can nestle bright red ornaments between the boughs.

PEPPER-CRUSTED PRIME RIB

Chapter 3

The Main Event

SHOWSTOPPING ROASTS, BUFFETS & TABLESCAPES

Holidays are a time to think big. A juicy turkey, succulent prime rib, a stunning crown roast, or a glistening ham are all suitably grand centerpieces for Christmas dinner. And when it comes to holiday buffets, you'll want delicious casseroles, and sandwiches to feed a crowd. In the pages that follow, we provide sure-to-please options.

Recipes

Crafts

Roasted Leg of Lamb with Pistachio-Mint Crust

To prevent the nut crust from burning, spread it over the roast after the lamb has cooked for one hour.

Active time: 30 minutes
Total time: 2 hours 45 minutes
Makes: 10 main-dish servings

1 whole bone-in lamb leg (7 pounds), trimmed
2 large garlic cloves, sliced
1½ teaspoons salt
2 tablespoons butter or margarine
1 small onion, chopped
1½ slices firm white bread, torn into ¼-inch pieces
½ cup shelled pistachios, finely chopped
2 tablespoons coarsely chopped fresh mint
¼ teaspoon coarsely ground black pepper
3 tablespoons all-purpose flour
1 can (14½ ounces) chicken broth plus additional ½ cup

1 Preheat oven to 325°F. Cut about 1 dozen ½-inch-long slits in lamb and insert slice of garlic in each. Sprinkle lamb with 1 teaspoon salt. Place lamb, fat side up, on rack in large roasting pan (17" by 11½"). Roast 1 hour.

2 Meanwhile, in 10-inch skillet, melt butter over medium heat. Add onion and cook until lightly browned and tender, about 10 minutes; remove from heat. Stir in bread, pistachios, mint, remaining ½ teaspoon salt, and pepper. At end of first hour of roasting, carefully pat mixture onto lamb.

3 Continue roasting lamb 1 hour 15 minutes to 1 hour 30 minutes longer, until meat thermometer inserted in thickest part of lamb (not touching bone) registers 140°F. Internal temperature will rise to 145°F (medium) upon standing. If well-done meat is preferred, continue roasting to desired doneness. When lamb is done, transfer to warm platter and let stand 15 minutes to set juices for easier carving.

4 Meanwhile, prepare gravy: Remove rack from roasting pan; pour pan drippings into 2-cup measuring cup. Add ½ cup of chicken broth to pan, stirring until browned bits are loosened from bottom. Add to drippings in cup; let stand until fat separates out. Place 2 tablespoons fat from drippings in roasting pan. Skim off and discard any remaining fat.

5 With wire whisk, whisk flour into fat in roasting pan over medium-high heat until well blended. Gradually whisk in meat juice and remaining broth and heat to boiling, stirring constantly; boil 1 minute. Pour gravy into gravy boat and serve with lamb.

Each serving: About 405 calories, 46g protein, 8g carbohydrate, 18g total fat (7g saturated), 0g fiber, 144mg cholesterol, 680mg sodium

Pepper-Crusted Prime Rib

Prime rib is a classic holiday entrée. While the roast rests, whisk together a simple cream sauce with roasted garlic and horseradish. No cooking required!

Active time: 15 minutes
Total time: 2 hours 10 minutes
Makes: 12 main-dish servings

1 (4-rib) beef rib roast (7 pounds), chine bone removed
2 tablespoons cracked pink or black peppercorns
2 teaspoons kosher salt
1 head garlic
½ teaspoon olive oil
½ cup reduced-fat sour cream
½ cup heavy cream
1 cup prepared horseradish, drained
¼ teaspoon salt
¼ teaspoon ground black pepper
Fresh dill sprigs for garnish

1 Preheat oven to 450°F. Place rib roast, fat side up, on rack in 14" by 10" roasting pan. Rub cracked peppercorns and kosher salt all over roast.

2 Cut top third off head of garlic, and keep both pieces intact. Drizzle oil over cut sides and place garlic top back on bottom. Wrap tightly in foil.

3 Place garlic on rack next to rib roast in oven. Roast both 20 minutes, then reset oven control to 350°F. Roast garlic 40 minutes longer, then unwrap and let cool. Roast beef 1 hour 30 minutes longer or until meat thermometer inserted into thickest part (not touching bone) registers 135°F. Internal temperature will rise to 145°F (medium-rare) upon standing. (If well-done meat is desired, continue roasting to desired doneness.) Transfer meat to large serving platter; cover loosely with foil and let stand 15 minutes for easier slicing.

4 Meanwhile, in medium bowl, with wire whisk, whip both creams together until soft peaks form. Press soft roasted garlic out of each clove into small bowl; discard skins. Add horseradish to garlic and mash with fork. Fold into cream mixture. Stir in salt and ground pepper. Spoon into small serving bowl. Garnish platter with fresh dill sprigs. Serve sauce alongside beef.

Each serving beef with 3 tablespoons sauce: About 690 calories, 40g protein, 4g carbohydrate, 56g total fat (24g saturated), 1g fiber, 162mg cholesterol, 550mg sodium

Pork Crown Roast with Apple-Pear Stuffing

For something different this holiday season, surprise your guests with this impressive pork roast featuring a fruity stuffing and cranberry sauce.

Active time: 45 minutes
Total time: 2 hours 20 minutes
Makes: 16 main-dish servings

1 tablespoon finely chopped fresh rosemary leaves
$2^1/8$ teaspoons salt
$2^1/8$ teaspoons ground black pepper
1 pork rib crown roast (9 to 11 pounds; see Tip)
1 bag (12 ounces) cranberries (3 cups)
$^1/2$ cup chicken stock
$^1/2$ cup apple juice
$^3/4$ cup sugar
2 teaspoons fennel seeds
2 Bosc pears, each peeled, cored, and sliced
1 pound apples, peeled, cored, and sliced
2 red onions, cut into thin wedges
1 teaspoon freshly grated lemon peel
Kale leaves and lady apples for garnish

1 Preheat oven to 425°F.

2 In small bowl, combine rosemary with 2 teaspoons each salt and pepper. Place pork on 18" by 12" jelly-roll pan and rub surface of meat all over with rosemary mixture. Roast 1 hour 30 minutes.

3 Meanwhile, in 4-quart saucepan, combine cranberries, stock, apple juice, sugar, and $1^1/2$ teaspoons fennel seeds. Heat to boiling on medium-high, stirring occasionally. Reduce heat; simmer 3 to 5 minutes or until cranberries just begin to pop. Remove from heat. With ladle, transfer $^1/2$ cup liquid from sauce to small bowl; set aside. In large bowl, toss pears, apples, onions, lemon peel, remaining $^1/2$ teaspoon fennel seeds, and remaining $^1/8$ teaspoon each salt and pepper to combine.

4 Reset oven control to 375°F. Roast pork 35 minutes longer. Carefully transfer fruit mixture to pan in even layer around pork, turning to coat with pan juices. Brush reserved liquid from cranberry sauce all over pork. Roast 10 to 45 minutes longer or until meat thermometer inserted in thickest part of pork (not touching bone) registers 145°F. (Internal temperature will rise 5°F to 10°F upon standing.)

5 Transfer roast to serving platter. With slotted spoon, mound pear mixture in center of roast (place any that will not fit on pork in serving bowl) and arrange some cranberries from sauce on top of pear mixture. Let stand 20 minutes.

6 Strain pan drippings into fat separator or medium bowl. Let drippings stand 1 minute to allow fat to separate from meat juices. Stir meat juices into cranberry sauce; discard fat.

7 Garnish serving platter with kale and lady apples. Serve pork roast with cranberry sauce and extra pear mixture, if any, alongside.

TIP: Around the holidays, crown roasts of pork are readily available in markets, but it's best to order a tied crown roast from your butcher ahead of time. Butchers trim crown roasts in different ways, so the roasting time varies widely. Be sure to use a meat thermometer to ensure perfectly cooked and juicy meat.

Each serving: About 495 calories, 45g protein, 22g carbohydrate, 25g total fat (9g saturated), 2g fiber, 128mg cholesterol, 460mg sodium

Pork Crown Roast with Apple-Pear Stuffing

Mustard-Glazed Fresh Ham with Cider Sauce

Cracklings, crunchy pieces of crisp, roasted pork skins, are a Southern treat. If you want to try them, cook them right along with the roast as directed below.

Active time: 20 minutes
Total time: 5 hours 20 minutes
Makes: 24 main-dish servings

1 whole bone-in fresh ham leg (15 pounds)
1 teaspoon Chinese five-spice powder (optional)
½ cup packed brown sugar
1 tablespoon dry mustard
1 tablespoon kosher salt
1 teaspoon coarsely ground pepper
¼ teaspoon ground cloves
2½ cups apple cider
Sprig rosemary for garnish

1 Preheat oven to 350°F. With knife, remove skin from pork, if any, and reserve. Trim excess fat from pork, leaving ¼-inch-thick layer of fat; discard. Place pork on rack in large roasting pan (17" by 11½"). Insert meat thermometer into thickest part of pork, making sure thermometer is at least ½ inch from bone. If you like, for cracklings, sprinkle reserved pork skin with five-spice powder. Place skin, fat side down, in 15½" by 10½" jelly-roll pan; set aside.

2 In small bowl, combine sugar, mustard, salt, pepper, and cloves. Rub mixture on top and sides of pork, pressing lightly with hand so it adheres.

3 Roast pork and skin in same oven 4 to 5 hours (16 to 20 minutes per pound; see Tip) or until meat thermometer registers 160°F and cracklings are browned and crisp. Internal temperature of pork will rise to 165°F upon standing. (Meat near bone may still be slightly pink.)

4 When roast is done, transfer to warm, large platter; let stand 20 minutes to set juices for easier carving. Remove cracklings from pan and drain on paper towels.

5 Remove rack from roasting pan. Strain pan drippings into medium bowl. Let stand 1 minute, until fat separates. Skim and discard fat. Return pan drippings to hot roasting pan; add cider and heat to boiling over high heat, stirring until browned bits are loosened from bottom of pan. Boil about 7 minutes or until sauce thickens slightly. Strain sauce into gravy boat or serving bowl. Makes about 2¾ cups.

6 Cut or break cracklings into serving-size pieces. Thinly slice roast and serve with cider sauce and, if you like, cracklings. Garnish with rosemary.

TIP: Roasting times for fresh ham can vary by as much as an hour, depending on whether the meat contains a basting solution or was previously frozen. The best way to make sure any meat is cooked to the proper temperature is to use a meat thermometer.

Each serving pork with 1 tablespoon sauce: About 340 calories, 30g protein, 7g carbohydrates, 20g total fat (7g saturated), 0g fiber, 107mg cholesterol, 300mg sodium

Each ¼ cup cracklings: About 130 calories, 7g protein, 0g carbohydrate, 11g total fat (4g saturated), 0g fiber, 19g cholesterol, 365mg sodium

Sage-Orange Turkey

This burnished bird is enhanced by a fragrant herb mixture cooked under its skin.

Active Time: 40 minutes
Total Time: 4 hours plus standing
Makes: 12 main-dish servings

1 fresh or frozen (thawed) turkey (12 to 14 pounds)
1 large onion (10 to 12 ounces), cut into 2-inch chunks
1/2 bunch fresh thyme
7 garlic cloves
1 large navel orange
1 small bunch fresh flat-leaf parsley
6 sprigs fresh sage
Pinch cayenne (ground red) pepper
4 tablespoons extra-virgin olive oil
1 1/4 teaspoons salt
3/4 teaspoon freshly ground black pepper
Sage sprigs, grapes, and clementines for ganish

1 Preheat oven to 325°F. Drain juices from turkey. Place giblets and neck in large roasting pan. Pat turkey dry with paper towels. Place turkey, breast side up, on wire rack in pan; fold wing tips under back of turkey. Scatter half of onion, half of thyme, and 2 garlic cloves in pan around turkey. Pour *1 cup water* into pan.

2 From orange, finely grate 2 teaspoons peel. Transfer peel to food processor along with 3 garlic cloves; pulse until garlic is finely chopped. Cut whole orange into 2-inch chunks and reserve. From parsley and sage, transfer 1 cup parsley leaves and 3 tablespoons sage leaves to processor; pulse until very finely chopped. Reserve herb stems. Add cayenne, 3 tablespoons oil, and 1/4 teaspoon salt to processor; pulse until well mixed.

3 Working from large-cavity end of turkey, gently run fingers between skin and meat to loosen skin from flesh on breast and legs. With hands, place herb mixture under skin on both sides of breastbone and on legs. Gently massage skin to evenly distribute mixture.

4 Rub 1/2 teaspoon salt and 1/4 teaspoon pepper inside body cavity. Place reserved orange and herb stems and remaining onion, thyme, and 2 garlic cloves in body and neck cavities. Fold neck skin under back of turkey; secure drumsticks together with kitchen string, band of skin, or stuffing clamp. Rub remaining tablespoon oil and 1/4 teaspoon each salt and pepper over turkey.

5 Cover turkey with loose tent of foil; roast 2 hours. Remove foil. If pan is dry, add *1 cup water*. Roast about 1 hour longer. Turkey is done when temperature on meat thermometer inserted into thickest part of thigh next to body (not touching bone) reaches 175°F and breast temperature reaches 165°F.

6 When turkey is done, carefully lift from roasting rack and tilt slightly to allow juices to run into pan. Place turkey on large platter and let rest.

Each serving turkey without skin: About 355 calories, 63g protein, 1g carbohydrate, 9g total fat (2g saturated fat), 0g fiber, 207mg cholesterol, 340mg sodium

Lemon-Roasted Chicken for a Crowd

When you need a dish for a holiday buffet but you don't have time to fuss, turn to this easy crowd-pleaser.

Active time: 20 minutes
Total time: 1 hour 50 minutes
Makes: 20 main-dish servings

1½ cups fresh lemon juice (from 7 large lemons)
¼ cup vegetable oil
1 large onion (12 ounces), finely chopped
2 large garlic cloves, crushed with garlic press
5 teaspoons salt
1 tablespoon dried thyme
2 teaspoons ground black pepper
5 chickens (3 pounds each), each cut into quarters

1 Preheat oven to 375°F. In medium bowl, combine lemon juice, oil, onion, garlic, salt, thyme, and pepper. In two large roasting pans (17" by 11½"), arrange chicken pieces, skin side up. Pour lemon-juice mixture over chicken.

2 Roast chicken, basting occasionally with pan juices, about 1 hour 30 minutes, rotating position of pans halfway through. Chicken is done when meat thermometer inserted in thickest part of thigh, next to body, registers 165°F to 170°F; breast temperature should reach 165°F.

3 Transfer chicken to warm platters. Skim and discard fat from drippings in pan; pour pan drippings into medium bowl. Spoon some pan juices over chicken and serve with remaining juices alongside.

Each serving: About 380 calories, 41g protein, 3g carbohydrate, 22g total fat (6g saturated), 0g fiber, 132mg cholesterol, 706mg sodium

Cornish Hens Milanese

Gremolata, a tasty Italian blend of chopped fresh parsley, freshly grated lemon peel, and pungent garlic flavors these rustic roasted hens.

Active time: 10 minutes
Total time: 1 hour
Makes: 4 main-dish servings

2 Cornish hens (1½ pounds each)
3 tablespoons chopped fresh parsley
1 teaspoon extra-virgin olive oil
¼ teaspoon salt
⅛ teaspoon ground black pepper
1 small garlic clove, minced
½ teaspoon freshly grated lemon peel

1 Preheat oven to 375°F. Remove giblets and necks from hens; reserve for another use. With poultry shears, cut each hen lengthwise in half. Rinse hen pieces with cold running water; pat dry with paper towels.

2 In small bowl, combine 2 tablespoons parsley, oil, salt, and pepper. With fingertips, carefully separate skin from meat on each hen half; spread parsley mixture under skin. Place hens, skin side up, in large roasting pan (17" by 11½").

3 Roast hens, basting with drippings three times, until juices run clear when thickest part of thigh is pierced with tip of knife, and instant-read thermometer registers 165°F when inserted into thigh, about 50 minutes.

4 Arrange hens on warm platter. In cup, combine remaining 1 tablespoon parsley, garlic, and lemon peel; sprinkle over hens.

Each serving: About 385 calories, 32g protein, 0g carbohydrate, 27g total fat (7g saturated), 0g fiber, 187mg cholesterol, 236mg sodium

BEST DO-AHEAD GRAVY

If you want to get a jumpstart on holiday prep, make this luscious gravy from turkey wings. You can refrigerate it up to three days.

Active time: 10 minutes • Total time: 1 hour 40 minutes • Makes: about 6 cups

1 tablespoon vegetable oil
2 turkey wings (1¹/2 pounds), separated at joints
1 large onion, quartered
2 large carrots, each peeled and cut into 4 pieces
2 large stalks celery, each cut into 4 pieces

1 garlic clove, sliced in half
4 cups chicken broth
3 cups water
¹/4 teaspoon dried thyme
¹/2 cup all-purpose flour

1 In deep 12-inch skillet, heat oil over medium-high heat until hot. Add turkey wings and cook 10 to 15 minutes or until golden on all sides. Add onion, carrots, celery, and garlic, and cook 8 to 10 minutes or until turkey wings and vegetables are browned, stirring frequently. Transfer turkey and vegetables to large bowl.

2 Add ½ cup chicken broth to skillet and stir until browned bits are loosened. Return turkey and vegetables to skillet. Stir in remaining broth, water, and thyme; heat to boiling over high heat. Reduce heat to medium-low; simmer, uncovered, 45 minutes. Strain into an 8-cup liquid measuring cup or large bowl; discard solids.

3 Let broth stand 1 minute until fat separates from meat juice. Spoon ¼ cup fat from broth into 2-quart saucepan; skim and discard any remaining fat.

4 Whisk flour into fat in saucepan and cook, stirring, over medium heat, until flour turns golden brown. Gradually whisk in reserved broth and cook until gravy boils and thickens slightly, stirring constantly. Pour gravy into 2-quart container or medium bowl; cover and refrigerate up to 3 days.

5 At serving time, reheat gravy and add pan drippings from roast turkey if you like.

Each ¹/4-cup serving: About 50 calories, 1g protein, 2g carbohydrate, 4g total fat (1g saturated), 0g fiber, 3mg cholesterol, 115mg sodium

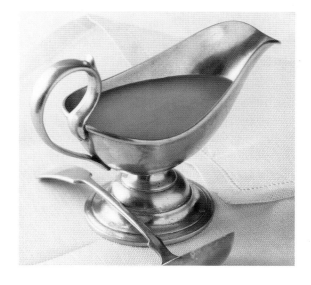

Italian-Spiced Shrimp Casserole

This quick but crowd-pleasing shrimp dish on rice gets its flavor from diced tomatoes and a variety of Italian herbs and spices.

Active time: 20 minutes
Total time: 40 minutes
Makes: 6 main-dish servings

1 cup long-grain white rice
1³/4 cups hot water
1 tablespoon olive oil
1 small onion, finely chopped
1 tablespoon fresh oregano leaves, minced
1/2 teaspoon crushed red pepper, or to taste
2 garlic cloves, crushed with garlic press
1 cup clam broth
1 can (14¹/2 ounces) no-salt-added diced tomatoes,
    drained well
1/2 teaspoon salt
1/2 teaspoon ground black pepper
1 pound 16- to 20-count shrimp, shelled and deveined, tail
    part of shell left on if you like
8 leaves basil, very thinly sliced, for garnish

1 Preheat oven to 400°F.

2 In 3-quart shallow baking dish, combine rice and water. Cover tightly with foil and bake 20 minutes.

3 Meanwhile, in 5- to 6-quart saucepot, heat oil over medium heat. Add onion, oregano, and crushed red pepper; cook 3 minutes, stirring occasionally. Add garlic and cook 30 seconds or until golden, stirring. Add clam broth and heat to boiling; reduce heat to medium-low and simmer, stirring occasionally, 6 minutes or until clam broth is reduced by half. Stir in tomatoes, salt, and black pepper. Remove from heat.

4 Arrange shrimp on top of rice in baking dish, in single layer. Pour tomato mixture evenly over shrimp; cover tightly with foil and bake 10 to 15 minutes or until shrimp turn opaque. Garnish with basil.

Each serving: About 245 calories, 16g protein, 35g carbohydrate, 4g total fat (1g saturated), 2g fiber, 93mg cholesterol, 300mg sodium

Salmon with Mustard Glaze

Let this luscious side of salmon star at your buffet—it takes only 30 minutes from start to finish.

Active time: 10 minutes
Total time: 30 minutes
Makes: 12 main-dish servings

2 lemons, thinly sliced, plus lemon wedges for garnish
1/2 cup spicy brown mustard
1/4 cup light mayonnaise
2 tablespoon sugar
2 tablespoons cider vinegar
1/2 cup loosely packed chopped fresh dill, plus additional
    for garnish
1 whole boneless side of salmon (3¹/4 pounds)
1/4 teaspoon salt
1/4 teaspoon freshly ground black pepper
³/4 cup reduced-fat sour cream

1 Preheat oven to 450°F. In 18" by 12" jelly-roll pan, arrange lemon slices in row in single layer from one corner to the diagonally opposite corner.

2 In medium bowl, stir mustard, mayonnaise, sugar, vinegar, and half of dill until sugar dissolves.

3 Place salmon, skin side down, on lemons in prepared pan. In medium bowl, set aside half of mustard mixture; spread remaining mixture on top of salmon. Sprinkle salt and pepper on top. Roast 13 to 15 minutes or until just opaque throughout (see Tip). Instant-read thermometer inserted horizontally into thickest part of salmon should register 145°F.

4 Meanwhile, stir sour cream and remaining dill into remaining mustard mixture. Place salmon on large serving platter; garnish with lemon wedges and dill. Serve salmon with sauce.

TIP: If you're lucky enough to be using wild Alaskan salmon in this recipe, the roasting time may be a bit longer than we specify.

Each serving: About 255 calories, 28g protein, 3g carbohydrate, 12g total fat (3g saturated), 0g fiber, 85mg cholesterol, 255mg sodium

BRUNCHES & BUFFETS

Overnight Savory French Toast

This cheese-crusted combo of bread, eggs, and Gruyère rests overnight so you can sleep in. In the A.M., pop it in the oven while you prep a salad or some fruit to serve alongside.

Active time: 20 minutes
Total time: 1 hour 15 minutes plus chilling and standing
Makes: 8 main-dish servings

6 large eggs
2 cups milk
1 tablespoon Dijon mustard
1/4 teaspoon salt
1/4 teaspoon ground black pepper
1/4 cup snipped chives, plus additional for garnish
1 loaf (9 ounces) French bread (preferably day-old), cut into 1/4-inch-thick slices
6 ounces Gruyère cheese, shredded (1 1/2 cups)

1 Grease shallow 1½-quart ceramic baking dish. In medium bowl, whisk eggs, milk, Dijon, salt, and pepper until well blended. Stir in chives.

2 Arrange half of bread in bottom of prepared baking dish, overlapping slices to fit. Pour half of egg mixture over bread and sprinkle with two-thirds of Gruyère. Cover with remaining bread, overlapping slices. Pour remaining egg mixture over bread; gently press down to help bread absorb egg mixture. Sprinkle with remaining Gruyère. Cover and refrigerate overnight.

3 Preheat oven to 350°F. Bake 50 to 60 minutes or until casserole is puffed and golden and tip of knife inserted in center comes out clean, covering top during last 15 minutes if browning occurs too quickly. Let stand 10 minutes to set custard before serving. Sprinkle with snipped chives.

Each serving: About 355 calories, 22g protein, 20g carbohydrate, 20g total fat (11g saturated), 1g fiber, 214mg cholesterol, 495mg sodium

Smoked Salmon Spread and Bagels

Instead of topping bagel toasts with large slices of expensive smoked salmon, treat your guests to this flavorful spread. It delivers big taste without the big bucks. Prepare the salmon spread up to one day ahead to give the flavors a chance to blend.

Active time: 15 minutes
Total time: 20 minutes plus chilling
Makes: 32 toasts

4 ounces Neufchâtel cheese, softened
4 ounces smoked salmon, chopped
1 container (8 ounces) reduced-fat sour cream
2 tablespoons fresh dill, chopped
1 tablespoon capers, drained and chopped
1/4 teaspoon salt
1/4 teaspoon ground black pepper
1 lemon
2 bagels, preferably sesame seed and poppy seed
1/2 small red onion, thinly sliced
1/2 English (seedless) cucumber, thinly sliced
4 red radishes, thinly sliced

1 In large bowl, stir cream cheese until light and fluffy. Fold in salmon, sour cream, dill, capers, salt, and pepper. From lemon, grate 1 teaspoon peel and squeeze 1 teaspoon juice; stir juice and peel into spread. Transfer to serving bowl. Cover and refrigerate at least 1 hour and up to overnight.

2 Preheat oven to 375°F. Cut bagels in half to form 4 crescents. Place bagel halves with cut side down, and cut each lengthwise into four slices to form 16 flat C shapes. Cut each in half crosswise to form 32 triangular shapes.

3 On large cookie sheet, arrange bagel slices in single layer; bake 8 to 10 minutes or until golden and crisp. Transfer to wire rack to cool completely.

4 Serve toasts with spread and onion, cucumber, and radish slices for topping.

Each toast with 1 scant tablespoon spread: About 35 calories, 2g protein, 3g carbohydrate, 2g total fat (1g saturated), 0g fiber, 6mg cholesterol, 140mg sodium

Country Captain Casserole

Though the exact origin of this well-known dish is often debated, its great flavor is never in dispute. It's sure to be well received on your holiday buffet.

Active time: 20 minutes
Total time: 45 minutes
Makes: 6 main-dish servings

2 tablespoons vegetable oil
2 green onions, thinly sliced, plus additional for garnish
2 cups long-grain white rice
3 cups water
4 carrots, peeled and cut into 1/4-inch-thick half-moons
1 large sweet onion (12 ounces), finely chopped
1 large yellow pepper (8 to 10 ounces), finely chopped
2 garlic cloves, finely chopped
1 tablespoon grated, peeled fresh ginger
1 tablespoon curry powder
1 teaspoon garam masala or ground cumin
2 cans (14 1/2 ounces each) no-salt-added diced tomatoes
1/2 cup golden raisins
1/4 teaspoon salt
1/4 teaspoon ground black pepper
1 1/2 pounds skinless boneless chicken thighs
1/4 cup sliced almonds, lightly toasted

1 Preheat oven to 350°F.

2 In 7-quart Dutch oven or other heavy, ovenproof pot with lid, heat 1 tablespoon oil on medium-high. Add 2 thinly sliced green onions and rice and cook 2 minutes or until onions soften, stirring. Add water and heat to boiling. Cover and bake 15 minutes.

3 Meanwhile, in 12-inch skillet, heat remaining 1 tablespoon oil on medium-high. Add carrots, onion, pepper, and garlic. Cook 6 minutes or until golden and tender, stirring occasionally.

4 Add ginger, curry, and garam masala. Cook 1 minute, stirring. Add tomatoes with their juice and raisins. Heat to boiling.

5 Sprinkle salt and pepper all over chicken. Add chicken thighs to pan, submerging in vegetable mixture. Heat

mixture to boiling and cook 2 to 4 minutes, or until chicken just loses its pink color throughout.

6 Uncover rice and pour chicken mixture over, spreading in even layer. Cover and bake 25 minutes longer. Garnish with almonds and additional chopped green onions.

Each serving: About 575 calories, 31g protein, 84g carbohydrate, 12g total fat (2g saturated), 6g fiber, 94mg cholesterol, 250mg sodium

Classic Italian Hero

Why pay more to buy a giant hero when you can put together your own and tailor it to taste? Whether you call it a hero, sub, hoagie, or grinder, this toothsome sandwich is a crowd-pleaser.

Total minutes: 15 minutes
Makes: 12 appetizer servings or 6 main-dish servings

1 large (16-inch) loaf Italian bread (12 ounces)
1/4 cup vinaigrette of choice
4 ounces thinly sliced hot and/or sweet capocollo, prosciutto, soppressata, and/or salami
4 ounces thinly sliced mozzarella cheese, preferably fresh mozzarella
Shredded romaine lettuce or arugula, peperoncini, basil leaves, roasted red peppers, very thinly sliced red onions, pesto, olivada, and/or sliced ripe tomatoes

1 Cut bread horizontally in half. Remove enough soft center from each half to make 1-inch-thick shell. (Reserve soft bread for another use.)

2 Brush vinaigrette evenly over cut sides of bread. Layer meats and cheese on bottom half of bread. Top with additional ingredients of your choice. Replace top half of bread.

3 If not serving right away, wrap sandwich in foil and refrigerate up to 4 hours. Cut into serving-size pieces and arrange on platter, or present whole sandwich on cutting board and let guests slice off desired amount.

Each appetizer serving: About 145 calories, 7g protein, 12g carbohydrate, 8g total fat (2g saturated), 1g fiber, 16mg cholesterol, 408mg sodium

Cheddar Grits Soufflé

Savory soufflé featuring grits and Cheddar cheese is a perfect brunch dish for special occasions.

Active time: 30 minutes
Total time: 1 hour 15 minutes plus cooling
Makes: 8 side-dish servings

6¹/₂ ounces extra-sharp Cheddar cheese, shredded
    (1¹/₂ cups)
2 cups water
2 tablespoons butter or margarine
¹/₂ teaspoon salt
2¹/₂ cups whole milk
1 cup quick-cooking grits
¹/₄ teaspoon freshly grated nutmeg
¹/₈ teaspoon cayenne (ground red) pepper
3 large eggs, separated
3 large egg whites

1 Preheat oven to 375°F. Grease 3-quart soufflé dish and sprinkle 2 tablespoons shredded Cheddar onto side.

2 In 4-quart saucepan, heat water, butter, salt, and 1½ cups milk to boiling on medium-high. Whisk in grits. Cover, reduce heat to low, and simmer 5 minutes or until thick. Whisk well, then whisk in nutmeg, cayenne, remaining 1 cup milk, and remaining Cheddar. Whisk in egg yolks; transfer to bowl and cool to room temperature.

3 In large bowl, with mixer on medium-high speed, beat all egg whites until stiff peaks form. Add one-third whites to grits mixture; beat until blended. Fold in remaining whites. Transfer to soufflé dish.

4 Bake 45 to 50 minutes or until puffed and golden brown on top.

Each serving: About 280 calories, 13g protein, 20g carbohydrate, 17g total fat (8g saturated), 1g fiber, 111mg cholesterol, 415mg sodium

Top: COUNTRY CAPTAIN CASSEROLE
Bottom: CLASSIC ITALIAN HERO

SETTING UP A CROWD-PLEASING BUFFET

Buffets have long been a popular and convenient way to feed a holiday crowd. The host sets out an assortment of dishes, along with serving utensils, dishes, and silverware. The guests line up and help themselves, moving from one end of the serving station to the other.

The advantages are many: The host can serve a large number of people at a relatively low cost while being freed up to join the party too. The guests can choose exactly what they want to eat and, because a buffet requires movement, they naturally mingle. It's casual entertaining at its best, but that doesn't mean it doesn't require some planning. Here are our tips on how to make it all come off without a hitch.

Choosing the Menu

Select dishes that can be cooked ahead and warmed for serving or partially prepared then assembled at the last minute. Casseroles are often a part of the menu, since they're cooked and served in a single dish that retains its heat. Limit the number of dishes you serve, but provide generous quantities of each: If guests return to the buffet for seconds, or even thirds, of your favorite family lasagna, you don't want them to wind up with an empty plate.

Make sure the entire main course and sides will fit on a single dinner plate. Food that you can eat with a fork—no large pieces that must be cut with a knife—are most convenient for the guests. You can certainly serve cakes, pies, or puddings for dessert, but cookies and fruit that can be eaten out of hand make it easy on both guests and host.

Setting Up the Buffet (and Routing Traffic)

A buffet can be set up in the dining room, living room, or kitchen on a table, on a sideboard, or even on top of a chest of drawers. The table can be set in the center of the room or pushed against a wall—the important thing is that guests can move around the table easily.

Arrange food and tableware so guests can serve themselves in a logical order, such as: napkin roll with utensils, dinner plate, hot dishes, cold dishes, salad, bread, and condiments. Be sure to place an appropriate serving utensil beside each dish, on a saucer to collect drips. Keep hot foods hot in a chafing dish or slow cooker. Warming the plates before service is always a nice touch. Can you use paper plates and cups and plastic utensils to save on dishwashing time? Yes, if it's an informal, family-style affair, although china and silver will make the meal holiday-special.

When the buffet is ready, invite guests to help themselves; offer to fix plates for elderly guests or children who may appreciate help. Replenish food when necessary, and invite guests to return for seconds.

Who Will Sit Where?

Unlike at a sit-down meal, buffet guests will load their plates and then settle in to eat on sofas, in armchairs, or even on the staircase, using any surface they can find—coffee tables, end tables, even their laps—to hold their plates. If there's room, or you invited a large crowd, consider setting up some folding tables in the living room, or even just folding chairs for extra seating.

Beverage and Dessert Stations

Set up a separate table for beverages, somewhat away from the main buffet. This not only reduces traffic jams, but also encourages guests to select their food at the buffet, then put down their plates before pouring drinks, maximizing ease and minimizing spills. A bowl of festive punch surrounded by punch glasses makes self-service especially easy. Check this station sporadically, replenishing ice, seltzer, and any mixers, and clearing any empty glasses that may have collected.

Desserts can also be set up on a separate buffet if you have the space. Put out serving dishes, coffee cups, and utensils pre-party, but wait until the main buffet is cleared to bring out the sweet stuff. Ask a friend to remove dinner plates while you clear the buffet table and reset it for dessert and coffee service—or arrange the desserts on a separate preset dessert buffet.

Pedestals are a great way to serve not only cakes and pies, but also cookies, bars, and candies: multi-layers of treats make for an eye-catching sweet finale. If you're serving coffee, a self-serve urn keeps it hot; provide hot water and assorted tea bags for tea drinkers, along with cream, sugar, and sliced lemons.

FESTIVE CENTERPIECES— IN 15 MINUTES OR LESS!

Centerpieces are usually last on the Christmas to-do list. Time is tight, the food comes first, and really, how different can a vase of flowers look each year? But this Christmas, you don't have to default to a boring, been-there bouquet, or leave a bare spot beside the breadbasket and hope no one notices—not when you can whip up any one of the following holiday-worthy centerpieces in fifteen minutes or less.

Whether you choose to display stalks of wheat, evergreens and berries, or an assortment of fresh fruit, the season's bounty plays a starring role.

1. Christmas Bulbs

Potted narcissus (see Tip), swaddled in burlap and tied with red twine, bring botanical beauty—and fragrance—to your dining room table or sideboard. Or use multiple pots to line a stairwell, as shown here. Time invested: five minutes. The payoff: a low-maintenance arrangement that'll stay fresh for several weeks.

TIP: Buy paperwhites from a florist, or force the quick-growing bulbs starting in mid-November. By Christmas, you'll have flowers that will bloom and perfume the air into the New Year. But paperwhites aren't the only potted plants available in late December; you can achieve a similar effect with pots of poinsettias, cyclamens, hollies, or even mini Christmas trees.

2. How Swede It Is

To make this no-fuss natural centerpiece, loosely cinch craft-store wheat stalks with red and white ribbon. Place faux snow inside a clear glass vase and nestle the bouquet of stalks on top. Surround with almonds in the shell and evergreen cuttings for easy organic elegance in under ten minutes.

3. Season's Bounty

A sap bucket is spray-painted red to add a hit of seasonal cheer, then filled to the brim with evergreen branches and berries. Total time—minus allowing the paint to dry!—twelve minutes. Purchase the holiday greens at a florist or select a loose assortment when your buy your Christmas tree; any variety of greens and berries will create a festive arrangement.

White burlap, bought by the yard and fringed at the ends, serves as an easy and affordable tablecloth. Here, its simplicity downplays the formality of the china and ornate dining table.

Chapter 4

Sideshows

SENSATIONAL SIDE DISHES & RELISHES

It's no secret that everyone relishes the sides as much as the turkey or roast. Our delicious recipes for potatoes, mushrooms, cranberries, and all the other trimmings are sure to please your crowd. And let's not forget the stuffing!

Recipes

Sour Cream Smashed Potatoes

Smashing small red potatoes with a combination of sour cream and milk yields a perfect texture and flavor. For color, garnish with chives.

Active time: 15 minutes
Total time: 1 hour 15 minutes
Makes: 12 side-dish servings

4 pounds small (not baby) red potatoes, well-scrubbed
2 teaspoons salt
1 cup whole milk
2 tablespoons butter or margarine
1 cup reduced-fat sour cream
1/4 cup snipped chives plus additional for garnish
1/2 teaspoon ground black pepper

1 In 8-quart saucepot, combine potatoes, 1 teaspoon salt, and *water* to cover; heat to boiling on high. Reduce heat to low; cover and simmer 45 to 55 minutes or until potatoes are tender when pierced with tip of knife. Drain well.

2 Meanwhile, in microwave-safe cup, microwave milk and butter on High 1 minute or until butter is melted and milk is warm.

3 Return potatoes to saucepot. With potato masher, coarsely mash potatoes with sour cream. Gradually add warm milk; continue to mash until potatoes are well blended but still slightly chunky. Stir in snipped chives, remaining 1 teaspoon salt, and pepper.

4 Spoon potatoes into serving bowl and garnish with additional snipped chives.

Each serving: About 185 calories, 4g protein, 32g carbohydrate, 5g total fat (2g saturated), 3g fiber, 11mg cholesterol, 295mg sodium

Braised Wild Mushrooms and Peas

An effortlessly elegant side that only tastes extravagant.

Active time: 15 minutes
Total time: 30 minutes
Makes: 12 side-dish servings

2 packages (10 ounces each) sliced white mushrooms
    (see Tip)
8 ounces shiitake mushrooms, stems discarded, caps cut
    into 1/2-inch-thick slices
8 ounces oyster mushrooms, tough ends trimmed,
    separated into lobes
1/2 cup water
2 tablespoons butter or margarine
4 green onions
1 package (16 ounces) frozen peas
1 tablespoon reduced-sodium soy sauce
1/4 teaspoon salt
1/2 teaspoon ground black pepper

1 In 12-inch skillet, combine all mushrooms, water, and 1 tablespoon butter. Cover and cook on medium 10 minutes. Uncover and cook 15 minutes or until mushrooms are tender and browned, stirring occasionally.

2 Meanwhile, finely chop white and pale green parts of green onions; thinly slice green tops, set aside. Stir chopped green onions and peas into mushroom mixture. Cook 2 to 3 minutes or until vegetables are heated through and liquid in pan returns to boiling, stirring occasionally.

3 Stir in soy sauce, salt, and pepper. Add remaining 1 tablespoon butter; stir until melted. Remove skillet from heat and stir in reserved sliced green onions. Transfer mixture to serving bowl.

TIP: We stretch the mushroom flavor by adding inexpensive white mushrooms to our mix of oysters and shiitakes. If you like, you can clean and sauté the mushrooms the day before, then just cover and refrigerate them. Reheat the mushrooms in a 12-inch skillet on medium before proceeding with step 2.

Each serving: About 80 calories, 5g protein, 11g carbohydrate, 2g total fat (0g saturated), 3g fiber, 0mg cholesterol, 175mg sodium

Sweet Potatoes with Marshmallow Meringue

To modernize this dish, we microwaved the potatoes before mashing and topped them with meringue mounds—a less-sugary substitute for the mini marshmallows made popular in the 1950s.

Active time: 30 minutes
Total time: 50 minutes plus cooling
Makes: 12 side-dish servings

3 pounds sweet potatoes
2 tablespoons pure maple syrup
1 tablespoon packed dark brown sugar
1 tablespoon fresh lemon juice
1/8 teaspoon ground allspice
1/4 teaspoon salt
3 large egg whites
1/4 teaspoon cream of tartar
1/3 cup granulated sugar

1 Prepare potatoes: Preheat oven to 400°F. Pierce sweet potatoes all over with tip of knife; place in large microwave-safe bowl. Cover with vented plastic wrap and microwave on High 15 to 17 minutes or until very tender when pierced with fork; drain. When potatoes are cool enough to handle, peel and return to bowl.

2 To bowl with sweet potatoes, add maple syrup, brown sugar, lemon juice, allspice, and salt. Mash with potato masher until smooth. Transfer potatoes to 2-quart casserole dish. (If making ahead, cover and refrigerate up to overnight; to rewarm potatoes, bake in 400°F oven for 15 minutes or until heated through.)

3 Prepare meringue: In large bowl, with mixer on high speed, beat egg whites and cream of tartar until soft peaks form. Sprinkle in granulated sugar, 2 tablespoons at a time, beating until sugar dissolves and meringue stands in stiff, glossy peaks when beaters are lifted.

4 Transfer meringue to large piping bag fitted with 1/2-inch plain tip or to gallon-size resealable plastic bag with one corner cut to form 1/2-inch hole. Starting at one side of casserole dish, pipe meringue in small mounds onto surface of sweet potatoes, covering entire surface. Bake 6 to 8 minutes or until meringue is golden.

Each serving: About 100 calories, 2g protein, 23g carbohydrate, 0g total fat, 2g fiber, 0mg cholesterol, 90mg sodium

Potato Gratin with Gruyère

This classic French side dish—made with nutty Gruyère cheese—is the perfect accompaniment to roasted meat or poultry.

Active time: 15 minutes
Total time: 1 hour 5 minutes
Makes: 8 side-dish servings

2 cups half-and-half or light cream
1/4 teaspoon cayenne (ground red) pepper
1 teaspoon salt
3 pounds Yukon Gold potatoes, peeled and thinly sliced
6 ounces Gruyère cheese, shredded (1 1/2 cups)

1 Preheat oven to 350°F. Grease shallow 8-cup baking dish. Set aside.

2 In 5-quart saucepan, combine half-and-half, cayenne, and salt; heat to boiling over medium-high heat.

3 Add potatoes and cook 2 minutes or until half-and-half mixture thickens slightly, stirring gently with heat-safe spatula.

4 Transfer half of potato mixture to prepared dish; sprinkle evenly with half of Gruyère. Top with remaining potato mixture and remaining Gruyère.

5 Bake 40 to 45 minutes or until potatoes are fork-tender and top is golden and bubbly.

Each serving: About 295 calories, 11g protein, 33g carbohydrate, 14g total fat (8g saturated), 2g fiber, 45mg cholesterol, 395mg sodium

Sweet Potatoes with Marshmallow Meringue

Wild Rice and Mushroom Stuffing

This recipe makes an elegant alternative to ordinary bread stuffing. It's richly flavored with two kinds of mushrooms and root vegetables. To make ahead, see Tip.

Active time: 40 minutes
Total time: 1 hour 30 minutes
Makes: 16 side-dish servings

1 cup wild rice (6 ounces), rinsed
3¾ cups water
1 cup dried cranberries or raisins
4 tablespoons butter or margarine
3 carrots, peeled and cut into ¼-inch dice
2 stalks celery, cut into ¼-inch dice
1 onion, cut into ¼-inch dice
1 teaspoon salt
½ teaspoon dried thyme
¼ teaspoon coarsely ground black pepper
8 ounces shiitake mushrooms, stems discarded,
　caps sliced
10 ounces white mushrooms, trimmed and sliced
2 cups long-grain brown rice
1 can (14½ ounces) chicken broth (1¾ cups)

1 In 2-quart saucepan, heat wild rice and 2 cups water to boiling on high heat. Reduce heat to low; cover and simmer until wild rice is tender, 35 to 40 minutes. Stir in cranberries; heat 1 minute. Drain wild rice mixture if necessary.

2 Meanwhile, in nonstick 5- to 6-quart Dutch oven, melt 2 tablespoons butter on medium heat. Add carrots, celery, and onion, and cook until tender and golden, 12 to 15 minutes. Stir in salt, thyme, and pepper, and cook 1 minute; transfer to medium bowl.

3 In same Dutch oven, melt remaining 2 tablespoons butter on medium heat. Add shiitake and white mushrooms, and cook until mushrooms are tender and golden, and liquid evaporates, about 12 minutes; transfer to bowl with vegetables.

4 Preheat oven to 325°F.

5 In same Dutch oven, heat brown rice, broth, and remaining 1¾ cups water to boiling on high heat. Reduce heat to low; cover and simmer until tender, 35 to 40 minutes. Stir wild rice and vegetable mixtures into rice.

6 Spoon stuffing into 13" by 9" glass baking dish or shallow 3½-quart casserole. Cover with foil and bake until heated through, about 20 minutes.

TIP: To cut down on last-minute cooking, prepare the components of this dish up to two days before serving. Increase the baking time to 1 hour or microwave until heated through, stirring once.

Each serving: About 120 calories, 3g protein, 23g carbohydrate, 2g total fat (0g saturated), 2g fiber, 0mg cholesterol, 190mg sodium.

Sausage, Chestnut, and Mushroom Stuffing

Prepare stuffing as directed in step 1, except use only 1 loaf bread. In step 2, omit oil. Remove casings from **1 pound sweet Italian sausage links**; cook meat in skillet on medium heat 10 minutes or until browned, stirring and breaking up sausage with side of spoon. With slotted spoon, transfer sausage to small bowl. Omit carrots and chop only **1 stalk celery**. Leaving sausage drippings in skillet, add onion and celery; cook 8 minutes. Stir in **1 package (10 ounces) sliced white mushrooms**, and cook 10 minutes or until golden. Omit parsley, poultry seasoning, and salt; stir in **¼ teaspoon dried thyme** with pepper. In step 3, to bread in bowl, add sausage, vegetable mixture, and **1½ cups chopped roasted, peeled chestnuts** along with broth. Complete recipe as in step 4. Makes about 12 cups.

Each 1-cup serving: About 270 calories, 10g protein, 26g carbohydrate, 14g total fat (4g saturated), 2g fiber, 30mg cholesterol, 620mg sodium

Cranberry-Cornmeal Biscuits

These drop-style biscuits complement any holiday meal. For a breakfast treat, serve with a softened sweet-cream butter and fruit preserves.

Active time: 15 minutes
Total time: 30 minutes plus cooling
Makes: 12 biscuits

1¼ cups cornmeal
¾ cup all-purpose flour
½ cup dried cranberries
2 tablespoons sugar
2 teaspoons baking powder
½ teaspoon salt
4 tablespoons butter or margarine, melted
¾ cup milk

1 Preheat oven to 400°F. Grease large cookie sheet.

2 In medium bowl, combine cornmeal, flour, cranberries, sugar, baking powder, and salt. Stir butter, then milk into cornmeal mixture just until mixture forms soft dough.

3 Drop dough by scant ¼ cups, 2 inches apart, on prepared cookie sheet. Bake biscuits 15 minutes or until golden. Cool biscuits slightly on wire rack to serve warm, or cool completely to serve later. Reheat before serving if you like.

TIP: To make ahead, wrap cooled biscuits in foil in a single layer. Leave at room temperature overnight or put in a resealable plastic bag and freeze up to 1 month.

Each biscuit: About 150 calories, 3g protein, 24g carbohydrate, 5g total fat (3g saturated), 2g fiber, 13mg cholesterol, 210mg sodium

Savory Bacon and Green Onion Scones

Who says scones have to be sweet? These are packed with crispy bacon and fresh green onion for bite. Serve up a basket at your holiday dinner or breakfast buffet.

Active time: 10 minutes
Total time: 25 minutes
Makes: 20 scones

6 slices bacon (6 ounces)
2 cups all-purpose flour
1 tablespoon baking powder
¼ cup finely chopped green onions
¼ teaspoon salt
¼ teaspoon ground black pepper
¾ cup milk

1 Preheat oven to 450°F. In 12-inch skillet, cook bacon over medium heat until browned. Reserve ¼ cup cooking fat. Drain bacon on paper towels; crumble.

2 Transfer bacon and and fat to large bowl. Add flour, baking powder, green onions, salt, and pepper, stirring to combine. Stir in milk.

3 Drop batter by heaping tablespoons onto ungreased cookie sheet. Bake 12 minutes or until golden brown. Serve hot, or rewarm in a 325°F oven 6 to 8 minutes before serving.

Each scone: About 90 calories, 2g protein, 10g carbohydrate, 4g total fat (2g saturated), 0g fiber, 6mg cholesterol, 175mg sodium

Savory Bread Stuffing with Pears

This golden brown stuffing is studded with pancetta, pears, fennel, and dried cranberries. No pancetta? No problem—just substitute an equal amount of bacon.

Active time: 25 minutes
Total time: 1 hour 25 minutes
Makes: 12 side-dish servings

1 large loaf (22 ounces) Italian bread (preferably day-old), cut into ½-inch cubes (14 cups)
2 tablespoons olive oil
3 ounces pancetta, cut into ¼-inch pieces
2 fennel bulbs (1 pound each), trimmed and chopped
1 large onion (12 ounces), chopped
2 garlic cloves, crushed with garlic press
2 Bartlett or Anjou pears, chopped
1 cup dried cranberries
3 cups reduced-sodium chicken broth
½ cup packed fresh flat-leaf parsley
1 tablespoon finely chopped fresh sage leaves
1 tablespoon finely chopped fresh rosemary leaves
½ teaspoon salt
½ teaspoon ground black pepper

1 Preheat oven to 400°F. Divide bread between two 15½" by 10½" jelly-roll pans or large cookie sheets and bake 15 minutes or until golden, rotating pans between upper and lower racks halfway through. Remove bread from oven; set aside to cool. Reset oven control to 350°F.

2 Meanwhile, in 5-quart Dutch oven or heavy saucepot, heat oil on medium-high. Add pancetta and cook 4 minutes or until golden brown and crisp, stirring occasionally. With slotted spoon, transfer pancetta to paper-towel-lined plate; do not remove Dutch oven from heat.

3 To same Dutch oven, add fennel, onion, and garlic. Cook 7 minutes or until vegetables are golden and tender, stirring frequently. Add pears and cranberries and cook 4 minutes or until softened, stirring frequently. Add broth and heat to boiling; reduce heat to medium-low and simmer 5 minutes.

4 In large bowl, combine bread and broth mixture. Stir in parsley, sage, rosemary, salt, pepper, and reserved pancetta. In shallow 3-quart glass or ceramic baking dish, spread mixture in an even layer. Cover with foil and bake 25 minutes. Uncover and bake 15 minutes longer or until top of stuffing is golden brown.

Each serving: About 275 calories, 7g protein, 46g carbohydrate, 7g total fat (2g saturated), 5g fiber, 5mg cholesterol, 515mg sodium

Savory Bread Stuffing with Pears

Roasted Acorn Squash

A traditional accompaniment to roasted turkey and pork, this squash side dish is as colorful as it is tasty.

Active time: 10 minutes
Total time: 40 minutes
Makes: 8 side-dish servings

4 small acorn squashes (1 pound each)
4 tablespoons butter or margarine, melted
¼ cup packed brown sugar
1 teaspoon salt
¼ teaspoon coarsely ground black pepper

1 Preheat oven to 450°F. Spray 15½" by 10½" jelly-roll pan with nonstick cooking spray. Cut each squash lengthwise in half; scoop out seeds and discard. Cut to make 16 equal-size wedges total.

2 Place squash pieces in pan. In cup, stir together butter, brown sugar, salt, and pepper. Brush cut sides of squash with butter mixture.

3 Bake 30 minutes or until lightly browned and fork-tender. (Let each person scoop tender flesh from wedges and discard skin.)

TIP: You can save time by cooking this squash in the same oven with one of our roasts. Just place the pan with the squash on the shelf below the meat for the last 30 minutes of the roasting time. While the roast rests, increase oven temperature to 450°F and cook squash another 10 to 15 minutes, until tender and browned.

Each serving: About 150 calories, 2g protein, 26g carbohydrate, 6g total fat (1g saturated), 3g fiber, 26mg cholesterol, 375mg sodium

Herb-Roasted Acorn Squash

Prepare as directed, but omit brown sugar and stir **2 tablespoons freshly chopped herbs,** such as rosemary, sage, or thyme, into butter mixture in step 2.

Pepper-Roasted Acorn Squash

Prepare as directed, but omit brown sugar and use **1 teaspoon black pepper** in step 2.

Spice-Roasted Acorn Squash

Prepare as directed, but add **1/2 teaspoon ground cinnamon** or **1/4 teaspoon ground nutmeg** to butter mixture in step 2.

Oven-Browned Carrots and Parsnips

This duet of sweet root vegetables is subtly accented by the flavors of fresh lemon peel and orange liqueur.

Active time: 20 minutes
Total time: 1 hour 20 minutes
Makes: 10 side-dish servings

2 pounds carrots, peeled and cut into 3" by ½" matchsticks
2 pounds parsnips, peeled and cut into 3" by ½" matchsticks
4 strips fresh lemon peel (3" by 1" each)
2 tablespoons orange-flavored liqueur
1 teaspoon sugar
½ teaspoon salt
¼ teaspoon coarsely ground black pepper
3 tablespoons butter or margarine, cut into pieces
Fresh parsley leaves for garnish

1 Preheat oven to 425°F. In bowl, toss carrots and parsnips with lemon peel, liqueur, sugar, salt, and pepper.

2 Divide the mixture between two 15½" by 10½" jelly-roll pans (or use 1 jelly-roll pan and 1 large shallow roasting pan) and dot with butter.

3 Roast vegetables until tender and browned, about 1 hour, stirring occasionally and rotating pans between upper and lower oven racks halfway through roasting time. Garnish with parsley to serve.

Each serving: About 135 calories, 2g protein, 24g carbohydrate, 4g total fat (3g saturated), 4g fiber, 9mg cholesterol, 190mg sodium

Roasted Acorn Squash

Ginger and Pear Cranberry Sauce

Cranberry sauce takes a walk on the spicy side with the addition of fresh ginger. Try the sweet orange marmalade variation, too.

Active time: 10 minutes
Total time: 20 minutes
Makes: 3 cups

3 Bosc or Anjou pears
1 bag (12 ounces) cranberries (3 cups)
1 tablespoon grated, peeled fresh ginger
3/4 cup sugar
1/4 cup water

1 Peel, core, and chop 2 pears and place in 3-quart saucepan. Add cranberries, ginger, sugars, and water and heat to boiling on high, stirring occasionally.

2 Reduce heat to medium and cook, uncovered, 5 to 7 minutes or until most cranberries pop and pears are tender, stirring occasionally.

3 Spoon sauce into serving bowl; cover and refrigerate 3 hours or up to 4 days. (Mixture will thicken as it chills.) Core remaining pear and cut into slices to use as garnish.

Each 1/4-cup serving: About 75 calories, 0g protein, 20g carbohydrate, 0g total fat, 2g fiber, 0mg cholesterol, 10mg sodium

Marmalade-Cranberry Sauce

Prepare cranberry sauce as directed above in step 1, except omit pears and ginger and use only 1/2 cup sugar. In step 2, cook only 3 to 4 minutes or until most cranberries pop. After removing from heat, stir in **1/2 cup sweet orange marmalade.** Complete recipe as in step 3. Makes about 2 1/4 cups.

Each 1/4-cup serving: About 105 calories, 0g protein, 27g carbo-hydrate, 0g total fat, 2g fiber, 0mg cholesterol, 25mg sodium

Citrus-Apricot Cranberry Sauce

Orange juice and apricots, fruits that were uncommon in most kitchens when this recipe first ran in the magazine in 1887, temper the tang of the cranberries in this easier-than-it-seems side—a single saucepan and some simmering is all it takes.

Active time: 5 minutes
Total time: 20 minutes
Makes: 3 cups

1 lemon
1/2 cup chopped dried apricots
1/2 cup orange juice
1/2 cup sugar
1/2 cup water
2 whole star anise
1/8 teaspoon ground black pepper
1 bag (12 ounces) cranberries (3 cups)

1 With vegetable peeler, remove all peel from lemon in strips; reserve strips and squeeze 2 tablespoons juice.

2 In 2- to 3-quart saucepan, stir together lemon juice, dried apricots, orange juice, sugar, water, star anise, and pepper. Heat to boiling over medium-high, stirring occasionally.

3 To saucepan, add cranberries and lemon peel. Return to boiling. Reduce heat to medium; simmer 3 to 4 minutes or until half of cranberries pop and mixture thickens. Let cranberry sauce cool before serving, or cover and refrigerate up to 4 days. Discard star anise and lemon peel before serving, if you like.

Each 1/4-cup serving: About 65 calories, 0g protein, 17g carbohydrate, 0g total fat, 1g fiber, 0mg cholesterol, 0mg sodium

CITRUS-APRICOT CRANBERRY SAUCE

Chapter 5

All Through The House

DAZZLING CHRISTMAS TREES, FESTIVE ORNAMENTS & STOCKINGS

There's no place like home for the holidays, especially when it's decorated with inspired touches brimming with Christmas spirit. We've rounded up our favorite ideas for brightening your hearth, plus a chorus of trees, from playful to regal to au naturel.

Crafts

HEARTH & HOME

Stockings are the most time-honored way to decorate the mantel, but why stop there? Our festive garlands, mini trees, and candles enhance the seasonal glow.

1. Give Them a Hand

Assist stockings with the annual gift-dispensing duties by transforming mittens into hanging holders for tiny treats—simply stitch on loops made from ribbons.

2. Sweater Stockings

A row of no-sweat sweater stockings—stitched up quickly from secondhand cable knits and Fair Isles— are ready to be stuffed with presents, while silver glass holders glow on the mantel (for safety, use LED candles).

To make these clever stockings, use old sweaters from your basement or a consignment shop. Create a stocking-shaped template in desired size—making sure to leave a ½-inch allowance for the seam. Cut out sweater for the front, and for the back, use felt in a corresponding color. Sew the two pieces right sides together, then turn inside out to finish. Sew a ribbon loop into the top for hanging.

3. Stocking Feat

Customized with an initial and brimming with greenery, a rough-hewn bootie adds primitive chic to a hearth or door. All it takes to make this folk-art facsimile: burlap, twine, and minimal sewing skills.

Create a stocking-shaped template and trace two stocking shapes onto white burlap. Cut out your shapes and, with right sides together, sew starting 3 inches down on both sides from the top (the top will fold over to make a cuff, as shown here). Turn right side out and press, creating the cuff. Fray the cuff edges by pulling at the loose threads of the burlap. Use twine to form a monogram letter and border at the top. Secure with a pin once you create a design you like, and sew in place. We threaded the twine through a dried orange slice for added interest.

Fill your new stocking with a layer of bubble wrap, to give it bulk and weight. Cut a manila folder or piece of stiff cardboard to fit in the top half, and place it behind the bubble wrap. Place a branch of spruce between the bubble wrap and folder, and add a few other light sprigs of seeded eucalyptus or other stocking stuffers of your choice. To hang, string a piece of wire through the back top of the burlap.

O, CHRISTMAS TREE!

Spruce it up! Create a personalized tree with handcrafted decorations, natural ornaments like pinecones and dried fruit, or a limited color palette ranging from regal jewel tones or greens and golds to classic red and white or preppy pink and lime green.

1 . Royal Highness
Rich jewel tones of violet, gold, blue, and green give this tree an air of royalty. A gold bead garland wraps it in luxury. To create a harmonious tableau, we extended the bold color palette to the under-the-branches display. The gifts are dazzling in violet and gold wrapping; a coordinating tree skirt ties it all together.

2. Have a Ball
Traditional Christmas tree ornaments have a whole life away from the evergreen. Display extra ornaments in clear glass bowls or in baskets, as shown here, for simple (and thrifty!) holiday decorating.

3. Tart and Tiny Tree
This tabletop feather tree is ripe with tiny lady apple, Seckel pear, and nut ornaments. Kumquat garlands wreath it with color. To make the playful tree topper, thread alternating kumquats and lady apples on thin wire and shape into a ring. A tableau of rustic pottery filled with fresh and dried fruit completes the look.

WEE TREES

Whether you live in an apartment that can't accommodate a full-size tree, or simply want to dress up a mantel or buffet, miniature tabletop trees are a fun and festive solution.

Artificial versions are available in a range of sizes, designs, and colors, online or wherever Christmas decorations are sold. Or purchase a small potted evergreen instead: Water it regularly and it will last into the new year. Miniature spruces look great in multiples along a mantelpiece or windowsill.

A wee tree requires wee decorations. Select tiny balls, colorful candies, or petite fruits, as shown in the Tart and Tiny Tree, opposite. For added sparkle, wind the branches with strands of Mardi Gras beads or small blinking lights.

4. Tree of Plenty

Set the scene for this Scandinavian-style tree with a smorgasbord of cool, crisp trimmings—from store-bought straw stars and mock cross-stitch ornaments to fabric caribou you can make yourself. Completing the look: A tree skirt of sheepskin and gifts wrapped in solid-hued paper.

5. Fit for a King Tree

A regal palette presides over this opulent tree, which pairs metallics with sapphire and amethyst hues. Instead of garlands wrapping around the tree, short strands of pearls, gold beads, and rhinestone spirals dangle from its branches. Candy-filled gold-paper cones are ornaments now, party favors later.

TREE-TRIMMING TOOL KIT

Get ready for the holiday season:

Keep the following tree-trimming essentials in a small toolbox to ensure the decorating process comes off without a hitch: wire cutter, glue, scissors, nylon fishing line, paper clips, narrow ribbon, and invisible tape.

1

2

3

4

5

ORNAMENTS WITH HOMEMADE CHARM

No need to spend a bundle on trimmings for your tree. You can make your own ornaments; inspiration—and instructions—provided below.

1. Woven-Ribbon Ornaments

Weave high-contrast ribbon to create these simple ornaments. Layer lengths within mini embroidery hoops, using double-stick tape around the inner hoop to hold the ribbon in place.

2. Clearly Christmas

For a fresh way to deck the halls, look no further than your own Tannenbaum to make these simple, stunning ornaments. Start by snipping sprigs of greenery off your tree and gathering some ribbon and red beads (these will be the berries). Purchase plain glass ornaments from a hobby store or online. Carefully remove the ornament tops, place the sprigs and beads inside, and replace the tops. Hang with ribbon, adding a holiday greeting on a strip of paper, if you like.

3. Cavorting Caribou

Follow our online template (goodhousekeeping.com/holidays/christmas-ideas) or draw your own to craft these charming fabric caribou. The star ornament above comes together in minutes with leftover wheat reeds, wooden craft shapes, a red marker, and some hot glue.

To make 24 caribou, you'll need ½ yard fabric, stiff iron-on fusible backing from a fabric store, wire for hanging, an X-Acto knife, and sharp scissors. Choose a cotton patterned fabric, and follow the manufacturer's instructions to iron it onto the fusible web. Download our pattern and trace it onto the back of the webbing. Using your sharp scissors, cut it out. Pierce a small slit on top of the caribou back with your X-Acto knife and slide a 3-inch wire through to create a hanger.

4. Smart Cookies

Classic store-bought butter cookies can easily become enticing ornaments. Purchase a box or tin of them plus narrow velvet ribbon; cut ribbon into lengths of about 10 inches. Fold each length of ribbon in half, making a loop, pull it through a cookie's center, and pull the ribbon's ends through the loop, knotting the ends. Just make sure to hang them out of reach of pets and hungry tykes.

5. How Sweet It Is!

Fill shiny gold cones with foil-wrapped *baci*—delectable Italian hazelnut-chocolate balls—and dangle them from your tree. To make the cones, cut out a semicircle of gold metallic poster board and staple to form a cone. Line the top edge with velvet ribbon (we used teal for contrast), then staple a gold ribbon on the cones to make a hanger. Then, most important, fill with chocolates.

6. Doves in Flight

These elegant three-dimensional birds, shown here on an evergreen wreath, are surprisingly simple to make. All you need is white printer paper, some scissors, and a pencil. For a template and instructions, visit goodhousekeeping.com/holidaycrafts.

Chapter 6

Sweet Finales

BEST-LOVED PIES, CAKES & COOKIES

Everyone at the table may say they're stuffed, but they'll always make room for dessert! Select a grand finale from our buffet of sweet and sensational options—or bake an assortment of cookies and other goodies so guests can indulge in more than one. From simple pies to a Chocolate Raspberry Roll, you'll find treats here to please both you and your guests.

Recipes

Crafts

Old-Fashioned Pecan Pie

Flaky homemade crust and copious amounts of dark corn syrup give this traditional pecan pie a leg up on the competition.

Active time: 25 minutes
Total time: 1 hour 25 minutes plus chilling and cooling
Makes: 10 servings

3/4 cup dark corn syrup
1/2 cup packed dark brown sugar
3 tablespoons butter or margarine, melted
1 teaspoon vanilla extract
Pinch salt
3 large eggs
1 1/2 cups pecan halves, toasted
9-Inch Baked Pie Shell, baked and cooled
  at least 10 minutes

1 Preheat oven to 350°F.
2 In large bowl, with wire whisk, mix corn syrup, sugar, butter, vanilla, salt, and eggs until blended. With spoon, stir in pecans.

3 Pour filling into baked pie shell. Bake 43 to 45 minutes or until filling is set around edge but center jiggles slightly. Cool on wire rack at least 3 hours for easier slicing. Refrigerate leftovers up to 1 week.

TIP: For a grown-up version of this classic, add 2 tablespoons bourbon and 1/4 teaspoon freshly grated nutmeg to the egg mixture in step 2.

Each serving: About 410 calories, 5g protein, 41g carbohydrate, 27g total fat (9g saturated), 2g fiber, 90mg cholesterol, 220mg sodium

Old-Fashioned Pecan Pie

Double-Crust Apple Pie

People with a passion for piecrust will appreciate this double-crust delight: Flaky layers of pastry encase a gently spiced apple filling. For a delectable tart-and-sweet flavor, use a mix of Granny Smith, Braeburn, and Golden Delicious apples.

Active time: 45 minutes
Total Time: 2 hours plus chilling and cooling
Makes: 10 servings

²/3 cup plus 1 teaspoon sugar
¹/3 cup cornstarch
¹/2 teaspoon ground cinnamon
¹/4 teaspoon nutmeg
¹/4 teaspoon salt
3¹/2 pounds Granny Smith, Golden Delicious, and/or Braeburn apples, each peeled, cored, and cut into 16 wedges
1 tablespoon fresh lemon juice
Unbaked dough for 9-Inch Double Piecrust
2 tablespoons butter or margarine, cut up
1 large egg white, lightly beaten

1 Place cookie sheet on rack in lower third of oven and preheat oven to 400°F.

2 In large bowl, combine sugar with cornstarch, cinnamon, nutmeg, and salt. Add apples and lemon juice, and toss to coat evenly.

3 On lightly floured surface, with floured rolling pin, roll larger disk of chilled dough into 12-inch round. Ease dough into 9½-inch deep-dish glass or ceramic pie plate. Gently press dough against bottom and up side of plate without stretching. Trim dough edge, leaving 1-inch overhang; reserve trimmings. Spoon apple mixture into piecrust; dot with butter.

4 Roll remaining disk for top crust into 12-inch round. Center round over filling in bottom crust. Trim pastry edge, leaving 1-inch overhang; reserve trimmings. Fold overhang under; bring up over pie-plate rim and pinch to form stand-up edge, then make decorative edge. Brush crust with some egg white. Reroll trimmings. With knife or cookie cutters, cut out apple and leaf shapes; arrange on pie. Cut short slashes in round to allow steam to escape during baking. Brush cutouts with egg white, then sprinkle crust and cutouts with remaining 1 teaspoon sugar.

5 Bake pie 1 hour 10 minutes or until apples are tender when pierced with knife through slits in crust. To prevent overbrowning, cover pie loosely with tent of foil after 40 minutes. Cool pie on wire rack 3 hours to serve warm. Or cool completely to serve later.

Each serving: About 455 calories, 4g protein, 61g carbohydrate, 23g total fat (11g saturated), 4g fiber, 39mg cholesterol, 330mg sodium

9-INCH BAKED PIE SHELL

Use this foolproof basic crust as the foundation for as many pies as you can dream up.

Active time: 20 minutes • Total time: 40 minutes plus chilling and cooling • Makes: 1 (9-inch) pie shell

1¹/₃ cups all-purpose flour
¹/₄ teaspoon salt
5 tablespoons cold butter or margarine, cut up

3 tablespoons vegetable shortening
4 to 5 tablespoons ice water

1 In food processor with knife blade attached, blend flour and salt. Add butter and shortening, and pulse until mixture resembles coarse crumbs. Sprinkle in ice water, 1 tablespoon at a time, pulsing after each addition, until large, moist crumbs just begin to form.

2 Shape dough into disk; wrap in plastic and refrigerate 30 minutes or overnight. (If chilled overnight, let dough stand 30 minutes at room temperature before rolling.)

3 Preheat oven to 425°F. On lightly floured surface, with floured rolling pin, roll dough into 12-inch round. Ease dough round into 9-inch glass or ceramic pie plate. Gently press dough against bottom and up sides of plate without stretching. Trim dough edge, leaving 1-inch overhang. Fold overhang under; pinch to form stand-up edge, then make decorative edge. Freeze pie shell 15 minutes.

4 Line pie shell with foil or parchment and fill with pie weights, dried beans, or uncooked rice. Bake 10 to 12 minutes or until beginning to set. Remove foil with weights, and bake 13 to 15 minutes longer or until golden. If shell puffs up during baking, gently press it down with back of spoon. Cool on wire rack until ready to fill.

9-Inch Double Piecrust

To make crust for a double-crust pie, increase ingredients to 2¹/₂ cups all-purpose flour, ¹/₂ teaspoon salt, 10 tablespoons cold butter or margarine, 6 tablespoons vegetable shortening, and 6 to 7 tablespoons ice water. Follow mixing instructions above, then divide dough into 2 disks, making one slightly larger. Follow instructions for rolling and baking dough for bottom crust, using larger disk. When ready to place top crust on pie, roll remaining disk into 12-inch round and proceed as recipe directs.

Each ¹/₁₀ pie shell: About 150 calories, 2g protein, 14g carbohydrate, 10g total fat (5g saturated), 1g fiber, 16mg cholesterol, 120mg sodium

Deep-Dish Baked Pie Shell

Prepare 9-Inch Baked Pie Shell as directed, but increase all-purpose flour to 1½ cups and vegetable shortening to ¼ cup. Ease dough into 9½-inch deep-dish pie plate.

Each ¹/₁₀ pie shell: About 165 calories, 2g protein, 14g carbohydrate, 11g total fat (5g saturated), 1g fiber, 16mg cholesterol, 120mg sodium

Cherry Hazelnut Linzer Tart

Here, sour cherry preserves step in for the more traditional raspberry filling. For a playful touch, we've decorated the top of the tart with stand-up Christmas tree cookies made from the tart dough.

Active time: 30 minutes
Total time: 1 hour 10 minutes plus chilling and cooling
Makes: 12 servings

2/3 cup hazelnuts (filberts, toasted, skinned, and cooled
1¼ cups all-purpose flour
¼ teaspoon baking powder
¼ teaspoon salt
½ cup butter (1 stick), softened (no substitutions)
½ cup granulated sugar
¼ teaspoon ground cinnamon
¼ teaspoon ground cloves
1 large egg, separated
1 teaspoon vanilla extract
1 cup sour cherry preserves
3 tablespoons confectioners' sugar

1 Preheat oven to 375°F.

2 In food processor with knife blade attached, pulse nuts, flour, baking powder, and salt until finely ground.

3 In large bowl, with mixer on medium-high speed, beat butter, sugar, cinnamon, and cloves 3 minutes or until pale and fluffy. Set aside 1 tablespoon egg white. With mixer on medium, beat in remaining egg white and yolk, then vanilla, until blended, occasionally scraping bowl.

4 With mixer on low speed, gradually add nut mixture. Beat 2 minutes or until blended. Transfer two-thirds of dough to 9-inch tart pan with removable bottom; transfer remaining to pastry bag fitted with ⅓-inch plain round tip. Press dough evenly into bottom and up side of pan. Freeze 20 minutes. Brush reserved egg white on bottom crust. Spread preserves evenly over tart. Pipe dough in bag in straight lines, 1 inch apart, across top. Pipe additional straight lines, 1 inch apart, diagonally over first lines to form lattice pattern. Bake 35 minutes or until browned.

5 Meanwhile, line cookie sheet with parchment. Transfer remaining dough onto sheet of waxed paper; cover with second sheet. Roll to ⅛-inch thickness. Freeze 5 minutes. With 2" by 1" tree cookie cutter, cut out as many cookies as possible; transfer to cookie sheet. Bake 7 to 9 minutes or until golden brown.

6 Cool cookies and tart in pan completely on wire racks. Remove side of pan. Dust cookies and tart with confectioners' sugar. Insert cookies upright into tart.

Each serving: About 265 calories, 3g protein, 38g carbohydrate, 12g total fat (5g saturated), 1g fiber, 38mg cholesterol, 120mg sodium

CHERRY HAZELNUT LINZER TART

Pumpkin Pie with Pecan Brittle

Pure pumpkin filling, rather than prepared pie mix, gives this pie its ultra-fresh taste. Wow guests by topping each slice with our easier-than-it-looks pecan brittle.

Active time: 25 minutes
Total time: 1 hour 40 minutes plus cooling and chilling
Makes: 30 servings

Pumpkin Pie
Deep-Dish Baked Pie Shell
³/4 cup sugar
3 large eggs
1 can (15 ounces) pure pumpkin (not pumpkin pie mix)
1 cup half-and-half or light cream
1¹/2 teaspoons pumpkin pie spice
¹/2 teaspoon salt

Pecan Brittle (optional)
¹/2 cup sugar
2 tablespoons water
2 tablespoons chopped pecans

Whipped Cream (optional)
¹/2 cup heavy or whipping cream
1 tablespoon sugar

1 Prepare pie shell. Cool on wire rack at least 10 minutes. Reset oven control to 350°F.

2 In large bowl, with wire whisk, mix sugar and eggs until blended. Mix in pumpkin, half-and-half, pumpkin pie spice, and salt until smooth.

3 Pour filling into pie shell. Bake 48 to 50 minutes or until edge is set but center still jiggles slightly. Cool pie completely on wire rack, about 4 hours to serve at room temperature. Or cool slightly, about 1 hour, then cover and refrigerate to serve cold later.

4 Prepare pecan brittle, if desired: Line large cookie sheet with foil; place sheet on wire rack. (Note: foil and cookie sheet will get very hot when topped with caramel.) In heavy 2-quart saucepan, heat sugar and water on medium heat until boiling. Cook about 5 minutes or until mixture turns golden. With heat-safe spatula, stir in pecans and cook 30 seconds. Working quickly and carefully, pour hot caramel onto foil and carefully lift and tilt cookie sheet slightly (holding foil in place) to spread caramel into a thin, even layer. Let brittle cool completely, about 30 minutes. When cool, peel foil away, and break brittle into 10 pieces to garnish pie.

5 When ready to serve, if you like, in medium bowl, with mixer on medium speed, beat cream with sugar until soft peaks form. Serve each slice of pie with a dollop of sweetened whipped cream, and garnish with a piece of pecan brittle. Refrigerate any leftovers up to 4 days.

Each serving without whipped cream and brittle: About 290 calories, 5g protein, 34g carbohydrate, 16g total fat (7g saturated), 2g fiber, 89mg cholesterol, 270mg sodium

Cranberry-Vanilla Cake with Whipped Cream Frosting

This pretty cake features three delectable layers slathered with a cranberry filling, all topped with gobs of creamy whipped frosting. To make it extra festive, we finished it with a candied cranberry garnish.

Active time: 50 minutes
Total time: 1 hour 40 minutes plus cooling and chilling
Makes: 16 servings

Vanilla Cake

3 cups cake flour (not self-rising)
1 tablespoon baking powder
¼ teaspoon salt
1 cup (2 sticks) butter or margarine, at room temperature
2 cups granulated sugar
5 large eggs, at room temperature
2 teaspoons vanilla extract
1¼ cups low-fat buttermilk

Cranberry Filling

1 bag (12 ounces) fresh or thawed frozen cranberries (3 cups)
1 cup granulated sugar
⅓ cup apricot jam
¼ teaspoon ground cinnamon

Candied Cranberry Garnish

¼ cup water
¾ cup granulated sugar
1 cup fresh or thawed frozen cranberries

Whipped Cream Frosting

2 cups heavy cream
1 cup confectioners' sugar
⅓ cup crème fraîche or sour cream
1 teaspoon vanilla extract

1 Prepare cake: Preheat oven to 350°F. Line bottoms of three 8-inch cake pans with parchment paper. Grease sides of pans and parchment. Into large bowl, sift flour, baking powder, and salt.

2 In large mixer bowl, with mixer on medium-high speed, beat butter and sugar until smooth and fluffy. Beat in eggs, one at a time, until incorporated. Beat in vanilla. Reduce speed to low; alternately add buttermilk and flour mixture in two or three parts, beating well after each addition.

3 Divide batter evenly among pans; smooth tops. Tap pans firmly against counter. Bake 40 to 45 minutes or until toothpick inserted in center comes out clean. Cool on wire rack 10 minutes. Invert cakes onto rack; remove pans and peel off parchment. Cool completely. Cakes may be wrapped in plastic and stored at room temperature up to 1 day.

4 Prepare filling: In 3-quart saucepan, combine cranberries, sugar, jam, and cinnamon. Cook on medium 8 to 10 minutes or until most berries burst, stirring often. Transfer to bowl; refrigerate until cold.

5 Prepare garnish: In 1-quart saucepan, combine water and ¼ cup sugar. Heat to boiling on high. Stir in cranberries. Cool completely, then drain. Place remaining ½ cup sugar on plate. Toss berries in sugar to coat. Place on wire rack; let dry 1 hour.

6 To assemble: Place 1 cake layer on cake stand; spread half of filling on top. Repeat with another layer and remaining filling. Top with third layer.

7 Prepare frosting: With mixer on medium speed, whisk cream until soft peaks form. Reduce speed to low; add confectioners' sugar, crème fraîche, and vanilla. Whisk until stiff peaks form. Spread frosting all over cake. Garnish with sugared berries. Cake can be covered and refrigerated up to 1 day. Remove from refrigerator 30 minutes before serving.

Each serving: About 590 calories, 6g protein, 85g carbohydrate, 26g total fat (16g saturated), 2g fiber, 137mg cholesterol, 300mg sodium

Sticky Toffee Bundt Cake

If you love traditional sticky toffee pudding, then you'll love this cake featuring the same flavors, including a gooey caramel glaze.

Active time: 35 minutes
Total time: 1 hour 40 minutes plus cooling
Makes: 16 servings

1 cup chopped pitted dates (5 ounces)
1 cup water
2 teaspoons ground ginger
1 teaspoon baking soda
2 cups all-purpose flour
1 teaspoon baking powder
1/8 teaspoon plus pinch salt
1 cup (2 sticks) butter or margarine, at room temperature (see Tip)
1 1/4 cups packed dark brown sugar
1 1/4 cups granulated sugar
3 large eggs, at room temperature
2 1/2 teaspoons vanilla extract
1 tablespoon light corn syrup
1/3 cup heavy cream
Red and green grapes for garnish

1 In 2-quart saucepan, combine dates and water. Heat to boiling on high. Remove from heat. Stir in ginger and baking soda. Cool completely.

2 Preheat oven to 350°F. Grease and flour 10-cup Bundt pan. Into large bowl, sift flour, baking powder, and 1/8 teaspoon salt; set aside.

3 In another large bowl, with mixer on medium speed, beat 3/4 cup butter and 1 cup each brown and granulated sugars until very well combined. Beat in eggs, one at a time, scraping side of bowl occasionally. Beat in 2 teaspoons vanilla extract. Add flour mixture and date mixture in alternation in two or three parts, beating well in between additions, until combined.

4 Pour batter into prepared pan. Bake 55 minutes to 1 hour or until toothpick inserted in center comes out clean. Cool in pan on wire rack 15 minutes. Invert pan onto wire rack. Cool completely. At this point, cooled cake can be wrapped tightly in plastic and stored at room temperature up to 1 day.

5 In 3-quart saucepan, combine corn syrup and remaining 4 tablespoons butter and 1/4 cup each brown sugar and granulated sugar. Cook on medium 3 minutes or until sugar has dissolved and syrup bubbles, stirring constantly. Stir in cream, remaining 1/2 teaspoon vanilla extract, and pinch of salt. Cook another 2 minutes, stirring constantly. Let cool 5 minutes.

6 Place sheet of waxed paper under cake. Pour caramel sauce over top of cooled cake and allow sauce to drip down sides. Let caramel set. Transfer cake to serving plate. Garnish with grapes.

TIP: If you're using margarine for the glaze, refrigerate it until it thickens before pouring it over the cake.

Each serving: About 355 calories, 3g protein, 54g carbohydrate, 14g total fat (9g saturated), 1g fiber, 72mg cholesterol, 265mg sodium

Chocolate-Raspberry Roll

This raspberry- and mascarpone-filled cake is our contemporary take on the traditional Bûche de Noël. The chocolate-frosted jelly-roll shape looks like a yule log; slicing it reveals a swirl of delectable raspberry filling.

Active time: 40 minutes
Total time: 55 minutes plus cooling and chilling
Makes: 12 servings

1 tablespoon water
1/3 cup plus 4 tablespoons granulated sugar
2 half-pints raspberries (6 ounces each)
6 squares (6 ounces) bittersweet chocolate, chopped
2 tablespoons butter or margarine
1/4 teaspoon salt
1/4 cup raspberry liqueur
6 large eggs, separated
3 tablespoons confectioners' sugar
1 cup heavy cream
1/2 cup mascarpone cheese

1 Preheat oven to 350°F. Grease 18" by 12" jelly-roll pan. Line with parchment paper; grease paper.

2 In medium bowl, stir water and 2 tablespoons granulated sugar. Fold in berries. Let stand while preparing cake.

3 Fill 4-quart saucepan with *2 inches water*. Heat to simmering. In large heatproof bowl, combine chocolate, butter, salt, and 2 tablespoons liqueur; set bowl over pan, stirring until smooth. Remove from heat. Stir in egg yolks, one at a time, beating after each addition.

4 In large mixer bowl, with mixer on medium-high speed, beat egg whites until frothy. Gradually add 1/3 cup granulated sugar; beat until stiff peaks form. Gently fold whites into chocolate, one-third at a time, until incorporated. Spread batter evenly in pan.

5 Bake 15 minutes or until toothpick inserted in center comes out nearly clean. Cool in pan on wire rack 10 minutes. Dust top of cake with 2 tablespoons confectioners' sugar; place sheet of waxed paper on top of cake. Set cutting board over cake, then flip board and pan together. Remove pan and peel off parchment. Cool.

6 In large bowl, with mixer on medium-high speed, beat cream and mascarpone until soft peaks form. Add remaining 2 tablespoons each granulated sugar and liqueur. Beat until stiff; spread over cake, leaving 1/2-inch border.

7 Starting from 1 long side, roll cake, peeling off paper in process. (Cake may crack slightly during rolling.) Place on platter, cover with plastic wrap, and refrigerate at least 1 hour or up to 1 day. (Refrigerate berries if making ahead.)

8 Dust with remaining 1 tablespoon confectioners' sugar. Serve with raspberries.

Each serving: About 305 calories, 6g protein, 26g carbohydrate, 22g total fat (12g saturated), 3g fiber, 139mg cholesterol, 115mg sodium

Christmas Fruitcake Drops

These colorful drop cookies boast an irresistible combination of coconut, chocolate, prunes, and cherries.

Prep time: 30 minutes plus cooling and setting
Bake time: 10 minutes per batch
Makes: about 36 cookies

1³/4 cups all-purpose flour
¹/2 teaspoon baking soda
¹/4 teaspoon salt
1 cup packed light brown sugar
6 tablespoons butter or margarine, softened
2 tablespoons vegetable shortening
1 large egg
1 cup pitted prunes, coarsely chopped
1 cup golden raisins
¹/2 cup red and/or green candied cherries, coarsely chopped
¹/2 cup flaked sweetened coconut
3 ounces white chocolate, chopped

1 Preheat oven to 375°F. Grease two large cookie sheets. In large bowl, combine flour, baking soda, and salt.

2 In another large bowl, with mixer on low speed, beat sugar, butter, and shortening until blended, occasionally scraping bowl with rubber spatula. Increase speed to high; beat until creamy, about 2 minutes. At low speed, beat in egg until blended. Add flour mixture, prunes, raisins, cherries, and coconut; beat just until blended.

3 Drop dough by rounded tablespoons, about 2 inches apart, onto prepared cookie sheets. Bake until edges are golden, 10 to 12 minutes. Cookies will be soft; with wide metal spatula, carefully transfer to wire rack to cool. Repeat with remaining dough.

4 In heavy small saucepan, melt white chocolate over very low heat, stirring frequently, until smooth. Arrange cookies on waxed paper and drizzle with white chocolate. Allow white chocolate to set, refrigerating if needed.

5 Store cookies in an airtight container up to 5 days, or freeze up to 3 months.

Each cookie: About 130 calories, 1g protein, 22g carbohydrate, 4g total fat (2g saturated), 1g fiber, 6mg cholesterol, 70mg sodium

Spritz Cookies

Spritz Cookies

Making these buttery molded favorites is easy with one of the new cookie presses, which offer cookie patterns for every holiday. You can sprinkle the cookies with coarse sugar before baking, or decorate afterwards.

Prep time: 35 minutes plus cooling and setting
Bake time: 10 minutes per batch
Makes: about 66 cookies

2¼ cups all-purpose flour
½ teaspoon baking powder
½ teaspoon salt
1 cup butter or margarine (2 sticks), softened
½ cup sugar
1 large egg
1 teaspoon vanilla extract
1 teaspoon almond extract
Candy décors (optional)
Ornamental Frosting (optional)

1 Preheat oven to 350°F. Place two cookie sheets in freezer.

2 On waxed paper, toss together flour, baking powder, and salt.

3 In large bowl, with mixer on medium speed, beat butter and sugar until pale and creamy. Beat in egg, then beat in both extracts. With mixer on low speed, gradually add flour mixture. Beat just until blended.

4 Spoon one-third of dough into cookie press or large decorating bag fitted with large star tip. Onto chilled cookie sheets, press or pipe dough into desired shapes, spacing 2 inches apart. Sprinkle with candy décors before baking, if using.

5 Bake cookies until lightly browned around edges, 10 to 12 minutes (see Tip), rotating cookie sheets between upper and lower oven racks halfway through. Place cookie sheets on wire rack to cool 2 minutes. Transfer cookies to wire rack to cool completely. Rechill cookie sheets and repeat with remaining dough.

6 Decorate cookies as desired with Ornamental Frosting, if using. Set aside to allow frosting to dry.

7 Store cookies in an airtight container up to 1 week, or freeze up to 1 month.

TIP: If you prefer your spritz cookies much lighter in color, bake them 5 to 7 minutes, until set but not golden.

Each cookie: About 50 calories, 1g protein, 5g carbohydrate, 3g total fat (2g saturated), 0g fiber, 10mg cholesterol, 20mg sodium

Coconut Macaroons

These flourless cookies are chewy and delicious (and a welcome treat for people who are allergic to wheat or gluten). Bag them in plastic, tie the packet up with a festive ribbon, and attach a gift card.

Prep time: 10 minutes
Bake time: 25 minutes per batch
Makes: about 42 cookies

3 cups sweetened flaked coconut
¾ cup sugar
4 large egg whites
¼ teaspoon salt
1 teaspoon vanilla extract
⅛ teaspoon almond extract

1 Preheat oven to 325°F. Line two large cookie sheets with parchment paper or foil.

2 In large bowl, stir coconut, sugar, egg whites, salt, and both extracts until well combined.

3 Drop dough by rounded measuring teaspoons, 1 inch apart, on prepared cookie sheets. Bake until set and lightly golden, 25 minutes, rotating cookie sheets between upper and lower oven racks halfway through. Set cookie sheets on wire racks to cool 1 minute. With wide metal spatula, transfer cookies to racks to cool completely. Store in an airtight container up to 3 days, or freeze up to 1 month.

Each cookie: About 40 calories, 1g protein, 6g carbohydrate, 2g total fat (2g saturated), 0g fiber, 0mg cholesterol, 32mg sodium

Peppermint Meringue Twists

Peppermint extract (and a little food coloring) lends these melt-in-your-mouth puffs a holiday twist. Peppermint oil will quickly deflate meringues. For these cookies, choose imitation peppermint extract instead.

Prep time: 1 hour plus standing
Bake time: 2 hours
Makes: about 12 cookies

4 large egg whites
¼ teaspoon cream of tartar
1 cup confectioners' sugar
¼ teaspoon imitation peppermint extract
Red and green food coloring

1 Preheat oven to 225°F. Line two large cookie sheets with foil.

2 In small bowl, with mixer at high speed, beat egg whites and cream of tartar until soft peaks form. Gradually sprinkle in sugar, beating until whites stand in stiff, glossy peaks. Beat in peppermint extract.

3 Transfer half of meringue mixture to another bowl. Using food colorings, tint meringue in one bowl pale red and meringue other bowl pale green.

4 Spoon red meringue into large resealable plastic bag and cut ¼-inch opening at corner. Repeat with green meringue and second bag. Fit large decorating bag (we used 14-inch size) with basketweave or large round tip (½- or ¾-inch opening). Place decorating bag in 2-cup glass measuring cup to stabilize, fold top third of bag over top of cup to keep top of bag clean. Simultaneously squeeze meringues from both resealable bags into decorating bag, filling decorating bag no more than two-thirds full.

5 Pipe meringue onto cookie sheets, leaving 1 inch between each meringue. If using basketweave tip, pipe meringue into 3- to 4-inch-long pleated ribbons, if using round tip, pipe 2-inch rounds.

6 Bake meringues 2 hours, carefully rotating cookie sheets between upper and lower oven racks halfway through. Turn oven off. Leave meringues in oven at least 30 minutes or overnight to dry.

7 When dry, remove meringues from foil with wide metal spatula. Store, with waxed paper between layers, in airtight container up to 3 weeks.

Each cookie: About 10 calories, 0g protein, 2g carbohydrate, 0g total fat (0g saturated), 0g fiber, 0mg cholesterol, 5mg sodium

German Chocolate Brownies

These brownies boast a chocolate base and a coconut-pecan topping. They're sure to delight any fan of their namesake layer cake.

Prep time: 25 minutes
Bake time: 45 minutes
Makes: 36 brownies

Brownie
1/2 cup butter or margarine (1 stick)
2 packages (4 ounces each) sweet baking chocolate
1 cup packed brown sugar
3 large eggs, lightly beaten
1 teaspoon vanilla extract
1 cup all-purpose flour
1/2 teaspoon salt

German Chocolate Topping
3 large egg whites
2 cups sweetened flaked coconut
1 cup pecans, toasted and chopped
1/2 cup packed brown sugar
1/4 cup whole milk
1/2 teaspoon vanilla extract
1/8 teaspoon almond extract
1/8 teaspoon salt

1 Preheat oven to 350°F. Line 13" by 9" baking pan with foil; grease foil.

2 Prepare brownie: In 3-quart saucepan, heat butter and chocolate over medium-low heat until melted, stirring frequently. Remove saucepan from heat; stir in brown sugar. Add eggs and vanilla; stir until well mixed. Stir in flour and salt just until blended. Spread batter evenly in prepared pan.

3 Prepare topping: In medium bowl, with wire whisk, beat egg whites until foamy. Stir in coconut, pecans, brown sugar, milk, vanilla and almond extracts, and salt until well combined. Spread topping over batter.

4 Bake until toothpick inserted 2 inches from edge comes out almost clean and topping turns golden brown, 45 to 50 minutes. Cool completely in pan on wire rack.

5 When cool, lift foil, with brownie, out of pan; peel foil away from sides. Cut lengthwise into 6 strips, then cut each strip crosswise into 6 pieces. Refrigerate in an airtight container up to 1 week, or freeze up to 3 months.

Each brownie: About 150 calories, 2g protein, 18g carbohydrate, 8g total fat (4g saturated), 2g fiber, 25mg cholesterol, 85mg sodium

QUICK & EASY COOKIE DECORATING

Like cheerfully wrapped packages, cutout cookies with bright trimmings are an essential component of any Christmas celebration. If you don't have time to pipe or paint intricate designs with frosting, here are some playful, easy techniques. These methods work their magic in minutes and are fun to do with kids.

1. Fast Frosting

Whisk 1½ cups confectioners' sugar with 1 to 2 tablespoons milk until blended; tint the mixture with your food coloring of choice and brush or pipe it on.

2. Luster Dust

Use a small artist's brush to paint the dust on a hardened iced surface. If you want only a pale shimmer, dip the brush in the dry luster dust powder and paint it onto the cookie. When subtle color with a metallic sheen is desired, mix ¼ teaspoon luster dust with ¾ teaspoon clear alcohol-based extract, such as lemon or almond. (Do not use water—the dust will be absorbed into the icing, leaving it sticky.) For more intense color, apply a second coat. Since extract evaporates quickly, work in small batches. (Note: Surfaces painted with luster dust dry in minutes.)

3. Piping Icing

You don't have to be a decorating pro to pipe simple designs on cookies. Thin the frosting with warm water to obtain the desired consistency. Then fill a piping bag or resealable plastic bag halfway with frosting. If you're using a plastic bag, use scissors to cut a ¼-inch opening off one corner of the bag. Squeeze the piping bag or plastic bag to create simple outlines or shapes on cookies.

4. Stenciling

Use a matte knife or single-edged razor blade to cut a small star, heart, or other desired stencil from lightweight cardboard. Place the stencil over a brownie or bar; sift confectioners' sugar, unsweetened cocoa, or cinnamon-sugar over the top. Carefully lift off stencil to reveal the design. Repeat with remaining bars.

5. Drawing with Frosting

Frost your cookies with a solid base layer. While the frosting on the base is still wet, fill a decorator's bag with stiff frosting and pipe concentric circles or parallel lines on the cookies. Then, working quickly, before frosting dries, draw a toothpick or the tip of a knife through the lines to create decorative effects as shown in photo.

6. Candyland

Frost cookies with store-bought frosting, then press on chocolate chips, miniature marshmallows, gumdrops, gummy candy, and other favorite candies to create tempting treats.

Chapter 7

The Holiday Wrap-Up

GOURMET GIFTS FROM THE KITCHEN & INSPIRED GIFT WRAPS

This year, do your Christmas shopping in your own kitchen. Create an assortment of enticing preserves, quick breads, and candies, then follow our tips for wrapping them in style. We guarantee these gourmet gifts will be received with delight!

Recipes

Crafts

Blushing Apple Butter

Cranberries tint this apple butter pink. Plan ahead: You can make a batch up to three weeks before the holidays and refrigerate it.

Active time: 30 minutes
Total time: 2 hours
Makes: 4 1/2 cups

3 3/4 pounds Granny Smith apples (8 large),
    peeled, cored, and thinly sliced
1 1/2 cups apple cider or apple juice
1 cup cranberries
3 strips (3" by 1" each) lemon peel
3 tablespoons fresh lemon juice
1 1/2 cups sugar

1 In heavy nonreactive 5-quart Dutch oven, heat apples, cider, cranberries, lemon peel, and lemon juice to boiling over high heat. Reduce heat to low; simmer, uncovered, 10 minutes or until apples are very soft, stirring occasionally.

2 Stir in sugar; heat to boiling over high heat. Reduce heat to medium; cook, partially covered, 1 hour or until apple butter is very thick, stirring occasionally (mixture may sputter and splash, so be careful).

3 Spoon apple butter into blender in small batches. Cover, with center part of lid removed to allow steam to escape (drape with clean kitchen towel to avoid splatter), and blend until smooth.

4 Spoon apple butter into jars and refrigerate, tightly covered, for up to 3 weeks.

Each 1 tablespoon serving: About 30 calories, 0g protein, 8g carbohydrate, 0g total fat, 0g fiber, 0mg cholesterol, 0mg sodium

Arrabiata Sauce

This piquant sauce is seasoned with crushed red pepper and ample garlic. The generous recipe yields enough for six 16-ounce jars for your friends and neighbors (with a little sauce leftover for you).

Active time: 15 minutes
Total time: 1 hour
Makes: 14 cups

½ cup extra-virgin olive oil
6 garlic cloves, crushed with side of chef's knife
4 cans (35 ounces each) Italian plum tomatoes
1 tablespoon salt
1 to 1½ teaspoons crushed red pepper

1 In 8-quart Dutch oven, heat oil over medium heat until hot but not smoking. Add garlic and cook, stirring, 2 minutes; do not brown. Stir in tomatoes with their juice, salt, and red pepper; heat to boiling over high heat. Reduce heat; simmer, uncovered, 50 minutes, or until sauce thickens slightly, stirring occasionally and crushing tomatoes with side of spoon.

2 For smooth, traditional texture, press tomato mixture through food mill into large bowl. Or leave sauce as is for a hearty, chunky texture. Cool sauce slightly then spoon into jar and refrigerate up to 1 week, or spoon into freezer-proof containers and freeze up to 2 months.

Each ¼-cup serving: About 30 calories, 1g protein, 3g carbohydrate, 2g total fat (0g saturated), 1g fiber, 0mg cholesterol, 230mg sodium

Pear Marmalade

Here, pears are combined with thinly sliced orange peel, fresh ginger, and a touch of allspice to make an unusually delectable marmalade. Use any variety of pear you like. The recipe yields seven 8-ounce jars: Friends and neighbors will be delighted to receive these preserves.

Active time: 30 minutes
Total time: 1 hour 30 minutes
Makes: 7 cups

PEAR MARMALADE

3 large oranges
6 pounds pears, peeled, cored, and coarsely chopped (12 cups)
2 tablespoons minced, peeled fresh ginger
4 cups sugar
⅓ cup fresh lemon juice
½ teaspoon ground allspice
7 half-pint canning jars and lids

1 From oranges, with vegetable peeler, remove peel along with some white pith. Cut enough peel into 2" by ⅛" strips to equal ¾ cup. Remove and discard seeds from orange flesh and coarsely chop enough to equal 1½ cups.

2 In heavy nonreactive 8-quart saucepot, combine pears, oranges and peel, ginger, sugar, lemon juice, and allspice; heat to boiling over high heat, stirring frequently. Reduce heat to medium-high; cook, stirring frequently, until mixture is very thick, about 45 minutes. With spoon, skim off any foam.

3 Spoon marmalade into jars and refrigerate, tightly covered, up to 3 weeks.

Each 1-tablespoon serving: About 45 calories, 0g protein, 11g carbohydrate, 0g total fat, 1g fiber, 0mg cholesterol, 0mg sodium

Freezer Strawberry Jam

If you're the super-organized type who starts planning Christmas in July, this recipe is for you. Peak-of-the-season farmstead berries make for a freezer jam that's fresh tasting even in December.

Active time: 35 minutes plus standing
Total time: 45 minutes
Makes: five 8-ounce containers

5 half-pint freezer-safe containers with tight-fitting lids
1 quart fully ripe strawberries, hulled
4 cups sugar
2 tablespoons fresh lemon juice
3/4 cup water
1 package (1 3/4 ounces) powdered fruit pectin

1 Prepare containers and lids (see Tip).

2 In large bowl, thoroughly crush enough strawberries to equal 2 cups. Stir in sugar and lemon juice until thoroughly mixed; let stand 10 minutes.

3 In 1-quart saucepan, combine water and pectin and heat to boiling over high heat. Boil, stirring constantly, 1 minute. Stir pectin mixture into fruit until sugar has dissolved and mixture is no longer grainy, 3 to 4 minutes. A few sugar crystals will remain.

4 Quickly ladle jam into containers to within 1/2 inch of tops. Wipe container rims clean; cover with lids.

5 Let stand at room temperature until set, about 24 hours. Refrigerate up to 3 weeks, or freeze up to 1 year. To use, place frozen jam in refrigerator until thawed, about 4 hours.

TIP: To store jam long-term in the pantry, you must sterilize the jars and lids. Wash the jars, lids, and screw bands in hot soapy water; rinse. Then submerge the jars in enough cool water to cover and heat to boiling. Remove the pot from the heat, cover it and let sit in the hot water for at least 10 minutes. Place the bands and lids in water and bring to a simmer (180°F). Remove pan from heat, cover, and keep hot until ready to use.

Each 1-tablespoon serving: About 45 calories, 0g protein, 11g carbohydrate, 0g total fat, 1g fiber, 0mg cholesterol, 1mg sodium

Fig and Walnut Cheese Ball

You can make these sweet-and-savory cheese balls up to a week ahead, but if you do, hold off on covering them with nuts—they will become soft and chewy. Instead, wrap the balls in plastic and refrigerate them, then roll them in chopped nuts just before gift giving.

Total time: 20 minutes plus chilling
Makes: 3 cheese balls or 24 servings

2 packages (8 ounces each) Neufchâtel cheese
1 cup dried Calimyrna figs (5 ounces), finely chopped, stems removed
1 cup freshly grated Parmesan cheese
2 tablespoons honey
1/2 teaspoon ground black pepper
1 cup walnuts, toasted and finely chopped

1 In medium bowl, with mixer on medium speed, beat Neufchâtel 1 minute or until fluffy. Reduce speed to low; beat in figs, Parmesan, honey, and pepper.

2 Place one-third of cheese mixture on sheet of plastic wrap and shape into ball; fold plastic up to enclose cheese ball. Repeat with remaining cheese mixture, making 3 balls. Refrigerate until chilled and firm, at least 1 hour or overnight. Roll chilled balls in chopped walnuts.

3 To serve, if cheese balls have been refrigerated overnight, let stand 30 minutes at room temperature or until soft enough to spread.

Each 1-ounce serving: About 120 calories, 5g protein, 7g carbohydrate, 9g total fat (4g saturated), 1g fiber, 18mg cholesterol, 155mg sodium

CAPE COD CRANBERRY LOAF

Cape Cod Cranberry Loaf

This classic cranberry bread makes a holiday-perfect gift, wrapped in cellophane and tied with a big bow.

Active time: 20 minutes
Total time: 1 hour 15 minutes plus cooling
Makes: 1 loaf or 12 servings

1 large orange
2½ cups all-purpose flour
1 cup sugar
2 teaspoons baking powder
½ teaspoon baking soda
½ teaspoon salt
2 large eggs
4 tablespoons butter or margarine, melted
2 cups fresh or frozen cranberries, coarsely chopped
¾ cup walnuts, chopped (optional)

1 Preheat oven to 375°F. Grease 9" by 5" metal loaf pan. From orange, grate peel and squeeze ½ cup juice.

2 In large bowl, combine flour, sugar, baking powder, baking soda, and salt. In small bowl, with wire whisk or fork, beat eggs, butter, and orange peel and juice. With wooden spoon, stir egg mixture into flour mixture just until blended (batter will be stiff). Fold in cranberries and walnuts, if using.

3 Spoon batter into prepared pan. Bake until toothpick inserted in center comes out clean, 55 to 60 minutes. Cool bread in pan on wire rack 10 minutes; remove from pan and cool completely on wire rack.

Each slice without walnuts: About 223 calories, 4g protein, 40g carbohydrate, 5g total fat (3g saturated), 2g fiber, 46mg cholesterol, 281mg sodium

Holiday Bread

This simple stollen, a quick version of the traditional sweetbread, makes a delightful holiday gift. Or serve it for breakfast on Chirstmas morning.

Active time: 10 minutes
Total time: 1 hour 5 minutes plus cooling
Makes: 1 loaf or 16 servings

2 1/3 cups all-purpose flour
1/2 cup sugar
1 1/2 teaspoons baking powder
1/4 teaspoon salt
1/2 cup cold butter or margarine (1 stick)
1 cup part-skim ricotta cheese
1 cup dried tart cherries or other dried fruit, coarsely chopped
1/3 cup pecans, toasted and chopped
1 teaspoon vanilla extract
1/2 teaspoon freshly grated lemon peel
2 large eggs
Confectioners' sugar (optional)

1 Preheat oven to 325°F. Grease large cookie sheet. In large bowl, stir together flour, sugar, baking powder, and salt. With pastry blender or using two knives scissors-fashion, cut in butter until mixture resembles fine crumbs. Stir in ricotta, dried cherries, pecans, vanilla, lemon peel, and eggs until well combined.

2 Turn dough onto lightly floured surface. With floured hands, gently knead two or three times to blend. With floured rolling pin, roll dough into 10" by 8" oval. Fold oval lengthwise, bringing top half not quite whole way over, so that bottom of dough forms 1-inch ledge.

3 Place stollen on prepared cookie sheet. Bake 55 to 60 minutes or until toothpick inserted in center comes out clean. Transfer to wire rack; cool completely. Sprinkle with confectioners' sugar just before serving if you like.

Each slice: About 205 calories, 5g protein, 27g carbohydrate, 10g total fat (5g saturated), 1g fiber, 48mg cholesterol, 165mg sodium

HOLIDAY BREAD

Overnight Sticky Buns

Not just sticky but also spicy, nutty, and downright delectable, these breakfast treats must be started the night before you plan to bake them. To give them as a gift, wrap securely in foil and tie with a bow.

Active time: 1 hour
Total time: 1 hour 30 minutes plus rising and chilling
Makes: 20 buns

Dough
¼ cup warm water (105°F to 115°F)
1 package active dry yeast
1 teaspoon plus ¼ cup granulated sugar
¾ cup milk
4 tablespoons butter or margarine, softened
1 teaspoon salt
3 large egg yolks
4 cups all-purpose flour

Filling
½ cup packed dark brown sugar
¼ cup dried currants
1 tablespoon ground cinnamon
4 tablespoons butter or margarine, melted

Topping
⅔ cup packed dark brown sugar
3 tablespoons butter or margarine
2 tablespoons light corn syrup
2 tablespoons pure honey
1¼ cups pecans, coarsely chopped

1 Prepare dough: In cup, combine warm water, yeast, and 1 teaspoon granulated sugar; stir to dissolve. Let stand 5 minutes or until foamy.

2 In large bowl, with mixer on low speed, blend yeast mixture with milk, butter, salt, egg yolks, 3 cups flour, and remaining ¼ cup granulated sugar until blended. With wooden spoon, stir in ¾ cup flour.

3 Turn dough onto lightly floured surface and knead about 5 minutes, until smooth and elastic, working in about ¼ cup more flour to keep dough from sticking.

4 Shape dough into ball; place in greased large bowl, turning dough over to grease top. Cover bowl and let dough rise in warm place (80°F to 85°F), about 1 hour.

5 Meanwhile, prepare filling: In small bowl, combine brown sugar, currants, and cinnamon. Reserve butter.

6 Prepare topping: In 1-quart saucepan, heat brown sugar, butter, corn syrup, and honey over low heat, stirring occasionally, until butter has melted. Grease 13" by 9" metal baking pan; pour brown-sugar mixture into pan and sprinkle evenly with pecans; set aside.

7 Punch down dough. Turn dough onto lightly floured surface; cover and let rest 15 minutes. On lightly floured surface, with floured rolling pin, roll dough into 18- by 12-inch rectangle. Brush dough with reserved melted butter and sprinkle with currant mixture. Starting at one long side, roll up dough jelly-roll fashion; place, seam side down, on cutting board. Cut dough crosswise into 20 slices.

8 Arrange slices, cut side down, on topping in baking pan in four rows of five slices each. Cover pan and refrigerate at least 12 or up to 20 hours.

9 When ready to bake, preheat oven to 375°F. Bake buns 30 minutes, or until golden. Immediately place serving tray or jelly-roll pan over baking pan and invert; remove baking pan. Let buns cool slightly to serve warm or cool completely and wrap tightly in foil to serve later.

Each bun: 290 calories, 12g protein, 5g carbohydrate, 12g total fat (5g saturated fat), 1g fiber, 50mg cholesterol, 195mg sodium

Overnight Sticky Buns

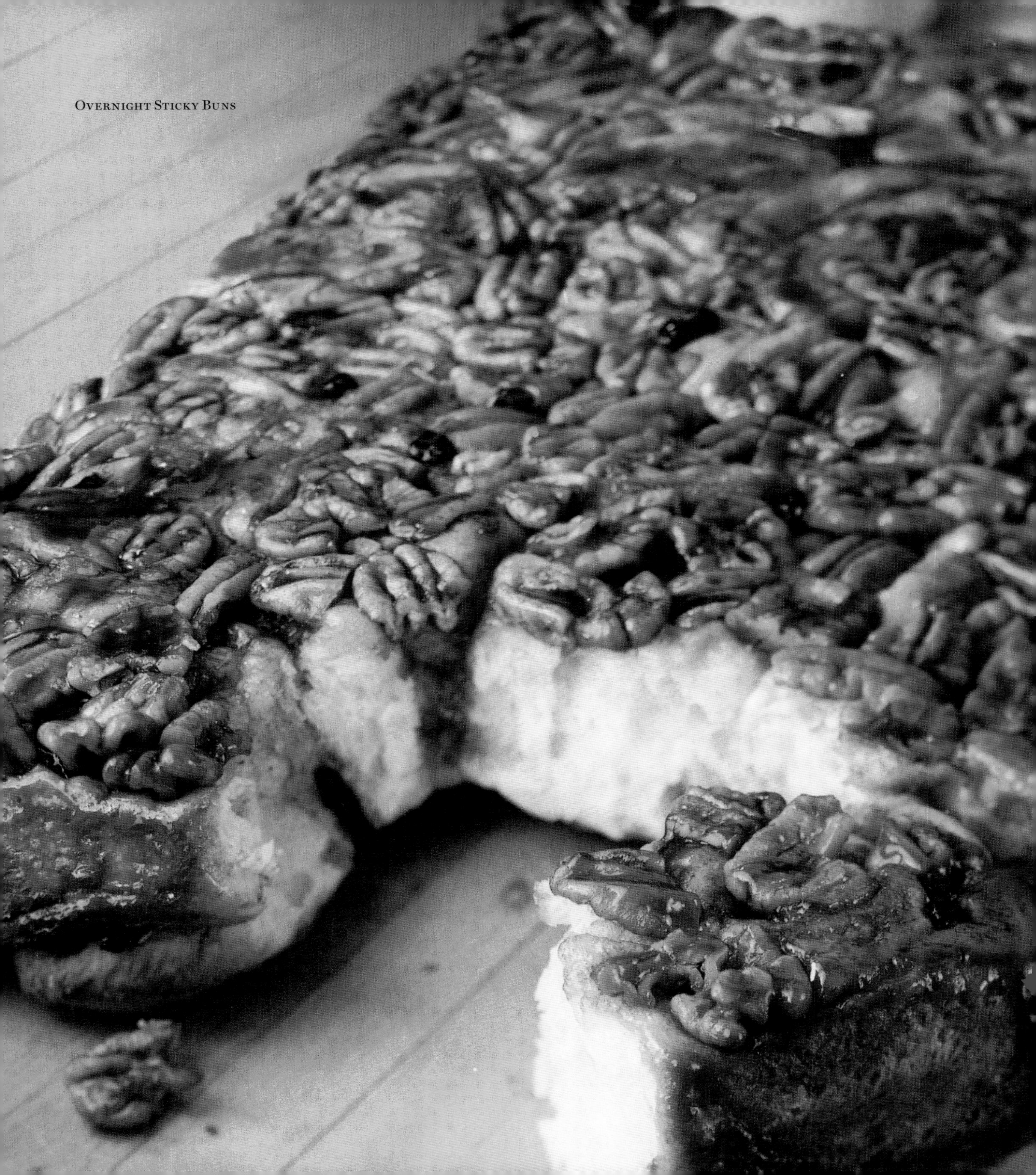

Chocolate Truffles

These bittersweet confections are easy to make—and a perfect gift for the chocolate obsessed. For extra flavor, you can add 2 tablespoons of liqueur, such as Amaretto, to the chocolate mixture.

Total time: 25 minutes plus chilling
Makes: 32 truffles

8 squares (8 ounces) bittersweet chocolate
1/2 cup heavy cream
2 tablespoons Amaretto or other favorite liqueur (optional)
3 tablespoons unsalted butter (no substitutions), softened and cut up
1/3 cup hazelnuts (filberts), toasted and finely chopped
3 tablespoons unsweetened cocoa

1 In food processor with knife blade attached, blend chocolate until finely ground.

2 In 1-quart saucepan, heat cream over medium-high heat to boiling. Stir in liqueur, if using; add mixture to chocolate in food processor and blend until smooth. Add butter and blend well.

3 Line 9" by 5" metal loaf pan with plastic wrap. Pour chocolate mixture into pan; spread evenly. Refrigerate until cool and firm enough to handle, about 3 hours.

4 Place hazelnuts in one small shallow bowl and cocoa in second shallow bowl. Set bowls near workspace.

5 Remove chocolate mixture from pan by lifting edges of plastic wrap and inverting chocolate block onto cutting board; discard plastic wrap. Using knife dipped in hot water and then wiped dry, cut chocolate mixture into 32 pieces. Quickly roll each piece into a ball. Roll half of balls in hazelnuts and other half in cocoa. Refrigerate truffles in an airtight container up to 1 week, or freeze up to 1 month. Remove from freezer 5 minutes before serving.

Each truffle: About 65 calories, 1g protein, 5g carbohydrate, 6g total fat (3g saturated), 1g fiber, 8mg cholesterol, 2mg sodium

Chocolate-Dipped Dried Fruit

Chocolate and dried fruit have a natural affinity for each other. We used dried apricots, apples, pears, and pineapple, but you can use other fruits, such as peaches and mango. Be sure to let the chocolate dry thoroughly before transferring the fruit to waxed-paper-lined gift boxes or tins.

Active time: 10 minutes
Total time: 15 minutes plus cooling
Makes: 33 pieces dipped fruit

4 squares (4 ounces) semisweet chocolate, chopped
1 teaspoon vegetable shortening
1 pound mixed dried fruit, such as apricots, apples, pears, and pineapple
3 ounces crystallized ginger (optional)

1 Place sheet of waxed paper under large wire rack. In top of double boiler or in small metal bowl set over 2-quart saucepan (double-boiler top or bowl should be 2 inches above water), melt chocolate and shortening, stirring frequently, until smooth.

2 With fingers, dip one piece of fruit at a time halfway into chocolate (see Tip). Shake off excess chocolate or gently scrape fruit across rim of double boiler, being careful not to remove too much chocolate. Place dipped fruit on wire rack; allow chocolate to set, at least 1 hour.

3 Layer fruit between sheets of waxed paper in an airtight container. Store at room temperature up to 1 week.

TIP: It's easiest if the larger pieces of fruit are dipped first. Use the smaller pieces to scrape up the melted chocolate remaining in the pan.

Each serving: About 55 calories, 1g protein, 12g carbohydrate, 1g total fat (1g saturated), 1g fiber, 0mg cholesterol, 2mg sodium

Pistachio and Tart Cherry Chocolate Bark

Pack this confection in decorative boxes lined with waxed tissue paper or colored cellophane. Make sure to note on the tag that this tart and nutty chocolate bark should be kept refrigerated until ready to enjoy, preferably no longer than one month for best flavor.

Active time: 20 minutes
Total time: 25 minutes plus chilling
Makes: 2 1/2 pounds

1 pound semisweet chocolate, coarsely chopped
8 ounces white chocolate, coarsely chopped
1 1/2 cups shelled pistachios, toasted
8 ounces dried tart cherries (1 1/2 cups)

1 Place semisweet chocolate in microwave-safe 8-cup measuring cup or large bowl. Place white chocolate in microwave-safe 2-cup measuring cup or medium bowl. Heat semisweet chocolate in microwave, covered with waxed paper, on High 2 to 3 minutes or until almost melted, stirring once. Remove from microwave and stir until smooth. Heat white chocolate in microwave, covered with waxed paper, on High 1 to 2 minutes or until almost melted, stirring once. Remove from microwave and stir until smooth.

2 Stir 1 cup pistachios and 1 cup cherries into semisweet chocolate; spread mixture to about 1/4-inch thickness on large cookie sheet. Spoon dollops of white chocolate onto semisweet mixture. With tip of knife, swirl chocolates together for marbled look. Sprinkle with remaining pistachios and cherries, and press lightly to make pieces adhere.

3 Refrigerate bark 1 hour or until firm. Break into pieces. Refrigerate in an airtight container up to 1 month.

Each 1-ounce serving: About 125 calories, 2g protein, 15g carbohydrate, 8g total fat (4g saturated), 2g fiber, 2mg cholesterol, 5mg sodium

PISTACHIO AND TART CHERRY CHOCOLATE BARK

1

2

CREATE A GIFT-WRAPPING STATION

Santa may have a whole workshop—and 364 days to prepare—but you don't. Here's how to handle the holiday present-wrapping rush:

Designate a table, then clear off the surface so you have ample room to spread out and a seat on which to perch. Gather tools that help you work efficiently, like a weighted tape dispenser for grabbing pieces of tape one-handed and sharp scissors (i.e., not the dull kitchen castoffs). Make a list of who's getting what, check it off as you wrap each gift, and finish each present with a well-secured gift tag (so your sister won't end up opening Grandpa's argyle sweater). Follow these tips for setting up a station that will make you a gift-wrapping machine.

1. On a Roll
Forget the frustration of tangled ribbon. Stack spools onto a paper-towel holder for easy access, and save leftover pieces of ribbon (that no longer have a spool) on empty paper-towel rolls, using a piece of tape to keep each wrapped tight. Stash the rolls in a handy box, so you know where to find them next year or whenever a wrapping project arises.

2. In the Bag
A hanging toiletry bag makes a perfect trimmings tool kit, since the clear compartments make your equipment accessible, and it can hang out (or get tucked away)

ALL WRAPPED UP
Forgo the fruitcake and give the hostess a package of present-wrapping fixings to help ensure that her holidays will be a little less frantic.

It's as easy as lining a decorative box with tissue paper and filling it with a variety of ribbons, gift cards, and tags, glitter, scissors, and snazzy gadgets like a ribbon curler and a pop-up tape dispenser. (You may want to buy a second set of tools to have at the ready in your own gift-wrapping station!)

KEEP VERSUS TOSS

· **Keep** wrapping-paper scraps for year-round use. Small sheets are perfect for creating custom gift tags, scrapbooking, and decoupage. Lay pieces flat (or carefully fold), and store in an expandable accordian folder near the rest of your wrapping supplies.

· **Toss** abused gift wrap (even if it's in a super-cute pattern), battered gift bags, and dog-eared boxes. If the packaging is mangled, it will only distract from your nice gesture. That said, wrinkled fabric ribbon can be saved: Iron it on low heat (you may need a spritz of water) to smooth it out.

· **Keep** unusual papers and trinkets. Recycle magazines and maps to swathe gifts, then salvage ornaments, costume jewelry, and tiny toys to tie on for a personal touch.

when not in use. Arm your arsenal with a hole punch, pen, glue stick, double-sided tape, scissors, gift tags, gift-topping embellishments, and some pretty premade bows.

3. Paper Chase

Corral rolls of wrap in a clean trash bin that you can stow in a closet when not needed. So papers don't unravel and rip, slip thin rubber bands (the thick ones can grab and rumple paper) around the tubes. Also, have some nonseasonal wraps in solid colors or simple patterns to get you through more than one holiday.

GORGEOUS GIFT WRAPS FOR SURE-TO-PLEASE PRESENTS

THE ULTIMATE GIFT-MAILING GUIDE

Can't visit all your loved ones? Send presents instead—the fastest, cheapest way. Here's how.

Pack Like a Pro

• **Pick the right-size box and don't overstuff;** if you do, the contents are likely to bust out before reaching their destination. Check the bottom flap of the box; it will tell you the maximum weight the container can bear.

• **When you're mailing multiple items, bubble wrap each separately,** then tape them together so they won't clank together during shipping.

• **Before sealing a package, give it a gentle shake.** If you hear anything moving, add padding—newspaper or shredded documents do the trick.

• **To make sure your box is fully reinforced, use the "H" method:** Tape along all the seams—it will look like there's an H on both the top and bottom of your box. And always use real packing tape; the other stuff won't hold up in transit.

Ship Smart

• **Reusing a box?** Strip off old labels, especially the bar codes, so the package doesn't get misrouted by the carrier.

• **Remove batteries** from toys and electronics, if possible. All the jostling can turn them on in transit, and they may burn out before arrival.

• **To make a package waterproof,** line it with a garbage bag.

• **The wrong zip code** can land a package back on your doorstep (weeks later), so check accuracy with the U.S. Postal Service's Zip Code Lookup tool at zip4.usps.com/zip4/welcome.jsp.

Weigh Your Options

• **Click on carrier's sites to schedule pickups.** UPS and FedEx charge for the perk; the U.S. Postal Service doesn't. Pay for postage online and print out shipping labels. To weigh a package at home: Stand on scale with your box, then without, and subtract.

• **Worried about weight?** The U.S. Postal Service has flat-rate boxes that you can fill with your heaviest items, then send to any state—all for one fixed price. (Check rates on shop.usps.com.)

• **Compare postage online** at shippingsidekick.com Enter the weight and destination of your package; the sites will give you rates for all the major carriers, including UPS and FedEx.

Beat Post Office Lines

• **If you decide to mail a gift at the post office,** avoid manic Mondays. (The first day of the week is typically the busiest for shipping).

• **Put minis in the mailbox.** A package weighing less than 13 ounces can be dropped in a mailbox.

Here a very Merry Christmas!

Susan

Have a very Merry Christmas!

1

To Sharon

2

3

4

If you usually just wrap your Christmas presents in red or green paper and call it a day, try these inspired designs, which go way beyond ordinary wrapping paper and ribbon. From rubber stamp monograms and a layered look to seasonal greenery and candy canes, these stunning presentations are (almost) as good as what's inside.

1. Candy Cane Christmas

Streamline gift giving by wrapping all your presents in the same pristine white paper, brightened with bold bursts of red and a hint of blue. It's elegant, economical, and easy to customize with tree cuttings, tags, and tempting candies.

2. Can Do

Make a gift card more personal by tailoring the wrap to the item. Here, a home-store certificate nestles in a prettied-up paint can. If you're giving a gift card for a manicure, use a cosmetics bag; for DVDs, try a popcorn box.

3. Play with Layers

Skip holiday-themed gift wrap and go with sweet stripes and cheerful checks. As long as the colors are coordinated, the more patterns you mix, the merrier.

4. Homespun Holiday Wrapping

With a little imagination, brown parcel paper, some twine, muted ribbon, and nature-made embellishments are all you need to wrap gifts. Here's how: Cover your presents in parcel paper; tie with twine or with ribbon in earthy tones. Then, for a burst of color, use floral wire to attach kumquats, holly sprigs, or other seasonal greenery or fruits to the packages.

REFRIGERATOR AND FREEZER STORAGE GUIDE

Get ready for the holidays: Maximize the longevity of your purchases by freezing them. To avoid freezer burn, leave as little extra air in the storage bag or container as possible. If you take a defrosting shortcut, like zapping edibles in the microwave instead of thawing them in the fridge, fully cook the food before refreezing it.

	WHAT TO SAVE	HOW LONG IN FRIDGE (set at or below 40°F)	HOW LONG IN FREEZER (set at or below 0°F)	HOW TO PACKAGE FOR FREEZING
FRUIT	Juices	Opened, 7 to 10 days Unopened, 3 weeks	8 to 12 months	Pour some off to leave room for expansion; reseal with masking tape; shake after thawing
	Bananas, ripe	2 week	8 to 12 months	In peel, in freezer bag (peel may discolor)
	Blackberries and raspberries	2 to 3 days	8 to 12 months	Spread on tray and freeze until firm; store in sealed container or freezer bag
	Blueberries	10 days	8 to 12 months	In original container, placed in freezer bag
	Cranberries	4 weeks	8 to 12 months	In original bag (if unopened) or freezer bag
	Grapes	1 to 2 weeks	8 to 12 months	See Blackberries, above (remove stems)
VEGETABLES	Broccoli and Cauliflower	3 to 5 days	Blanched for 3 minutes, 8 to 12 months*	In freezer bag
	Cabbage (shredded or cut into 1½-inch pieces)	1 week	Blanched for 1½ minutes, 8 to 12 months*	In freezer bag
	Carrots (cut into ¼-inch cubes)	2 weeks	Blanched for 2 minutes, 8 to 12 months*	In freezer bag
	Corn (off the cob)	2 weeks	Blanched for 2 minutes, 8 to 12 months*	In freezer bag
	Green beans (trimmed)	1 week	Blanched for 3 minutes, 8 to 12 months*	In freezer bag
	Potatoes, small (peeled)	No (they discolor and change flavor)	Blanched for 3 to 5 minutes, 8 to 12 months	In freezer bag

*To blanch vegetables, cook in rapidly boiling water for recommended time. Then cool quickly in ice water bath and drain well. This slows or stops action of enzymes that can cause loss of flavor, color, and texture. Cook frozen vegetables without thawing.

WHAT TO SAVE	HOW LONG IN FRIDGE (set at or below 40°F)	HOW LONG IN FREEZER (set at or below 0°F)	HOW TO PACKAGE FOR FREEZING
Steaks	3 to 5 days	10 to 12 months	In freezer bag
Chops	3 to 5 days	4 to 6 months	In freezer bag
Roasts	3 to 5 days	10 to 12 months	In freezer bag
Ham, full cooked (whole, half, slices)	Opened, 5 days In vacumn package, 1 month	1 to 2 months	In freezer bag
Ground	1 to 2 days	3 to 4 months	In freezer bag
Sausages, raw	1 to 2 days	1 to 2 months	In freezer bag
Sausages, fully cooked	Opened, 1 week Unopened, 2 weeks	1 to 2 months (opened or unopened)	In original packaging, placed in freezer bag
Bacon	1 week	1 month (opened or unopened)	In original packaging, placed in freezer bag
Casseroles, cooked, meat	2 to 3 days	2 to 3 months	In casserole dish, then remove from dish and transfer to freezer bag
Whole	1 to 2 days	1 year	In freezer bag
Pieces	1 to 2 days	9 months	In freezer bag
Ground	1 to 2 days	3 to 4 months	In freezer bag
Sausages, raw	1 to 2 days	1 to 2 months	In freezer bag
Casseroles, cooked, poultry	2 to 3 days	2 to 3 months	In casserole dish, then remove from dish and transfer to freezer bag
Lean (such as cod, sole, flounder)	1 to 2 days	3 to 6 months	In freezer bag
Oily (such as salmon)	1 to 2 days	2 to 3 months	In freezer bag
Smoked (such as salmon in vacuum pack)	Opened, 3 to 5 days Unopened, 1 month	2 months	Place original package in freezer bag
Shellfish (such as shrimp and shucked oysters, scallops, mussels)	1 to 2 days unshucked	3 months shucked	In freezer bag

MEAT

POULTRY

FISH

WHAT TO SAVE	HOW LONG IN FRIDGE (set at or below 40°F)	HOW LONG IN FREEZER (set at or below 0°F)	HOW TO PACKAGE FOR FREEZING
DAIRY			
Cheese, grated	1 month	3 to 4 months	In freezer bag
Hard cheeses, in blocks (such as Cheddar, Swiss, Parmesan)	Opened, 3 to 4 months Unopened, 6 months	6 months	Cut into smaller portions, wrap each portion in plastic wrap, then place in freezer bag
Soft cheeses (such as Brie, feta, goat)	2 weeks	6 months	See Hard cheeses, in blocks, above
Butter	2 to 3 months	6 to 9 months	For a month or less, in original packaging For longer term, in freezer bag
Egg whites or yolks; beaten eggs	2 to 4 days	6 months	In sealed container closest in volume to amount you're storing; label with number of eggs inside
Milk	1 week	6 months	See Juices
Cream, heavy cream	Opened, 1 week	6 months (only heavy cream freezes well)	See Juices
BAKED GOODS			
Breads and rolls, yeast	No (refrigeration makes bread go stale quickly)	3 to 6 months	In original package, then wrapped with foil or plastic wrap, or in freezer bag
Breads, quick (such as zucchini bread, biscuits, or scones)	No (refrigeration makes bread go stale quickly)	3 to 6 months	In freezer bag
Cookies, baked	3 to 5 days (depends on type of cookie)	3 months	In container, separated by layers of waxed paper if frosted or fragile
Cookie dough, raw	1 to 2 days (wrap in plastic)	2 to 3 months	Wrap in plastic wrap, then place in freezer bag
Brownies and bars	2 to 5 days (depends on type of bar)	3 months	Slice bars and place in container, separated by layers of waxed paper
Pies, fruit, unbaked	1 day	2 to 3 months	Wrap pie and pan in plastic, then place in freezer bag
Piecrust, raw	3 to 4 days (rolled in ball and wrapped in plastic)	2 to 3 months	Roll in ball and wrap in plastic, then place in freezer bag

EMERGENCY BAKING SUBSTITUTIONS

Baking powder, 1 teaspoon
Use ½ teaspoon cream of tartar and ¼ teaspoon baking soda (make fresh for each use).

Buttermilk, 1 cup
Place 1 tablespoon vinegar or lemon juice in cup and stir in enough mwilk to equal 1 cup; let stand 5 minutes to thicken. Or use 1 cup plain yogurt or sour cream thinned with ¼ cup milk (there will be some left over).

Cake flour, 1 cup
Place 2 tablespoons cornstarch in cup and add enough all-purpose flour to fill to overflowing; level off top; stir well before using.

Chocolate, semisweet, melted 1 ounce
Use ½ ounce unsweetened chocolate plus 1 tablespoon granulated sugar

Chocolate, unsweetened, melted, 1 ounce
Use 3 tablespoons unsweetened cocoa plus 1 tablespoon vegetable oil, shortening, butter, or margarine.

Cornstarch (for thickening), 1 tablespoon
Use 2 tablespoons all-purpose flour, quick-cooking tapioca, or arrowroot.

Corn syrup, light or dark, 1 cup
1¼ cups granulated or packed brown sugar plus ¼ cup liquid (use whatever liquid the recipe already calls for)

Half-and-Half, 1 cup
Use ⅞ cup whole milk plus 1½ tablespoons butter, or ½ cup light cream plus ½ cup whole milk.

Light brown sugar, 1 cup
Use 1 cup granulated sugar and 1 tablespoon molasses, or use dark brown sugar.

Milk, whole, 1 cup
Use 1 cup nonfat milk plus 2 teaspoons butter or margarine or ½ cup evaporated whole milk plus ½ cup water.

Pine nuts
Use walnuts or almonds.

Sour Cream, 1 cup
Use 1 cup plain yogurt, or ¾ cup sour milk, buttermilk or plain yogurt plus ⅓ cup butter, or 1 tablespoon lemon juice plus evaporated whole milk to equal 1 cup

Yeast, active dry, 1/4-ounce package
Use 0.6-ounce cake, or use one third of 2-ounce cake compressed yeast.

Vanilla extract
Use brandy or an appropriately flavored liqueur.

Whipping Cream (36-40% fat), 1 cup
Use ¾ cup whole milk plus ⅓ cup melted butter. Use this for baking purposes, not for topping.

INDEX

Note: Page numbers in *italics* indicate photographs on pages separate from recipes or crafts.

PHOTOGRAPHY CREDITS

The Good Housekeeping Triple-Test Promise

At *Good Housekeeping*, we want to make sure that every recipe we print works in any oven, with any brand of ingredient, no matter what. That's why, in our test kitchens at the **Good Housekeeping Research Institute**, we go all out: We test each recipe at least three times—and, often, several more times after that.

When a recipe is first developed, one member of our team prepares the dish and we judge it on these criteria: It must be **delicious, family-friendly, healthy,** and **easy to make.**

1 The recipe is then tested several more times to fine-tune the flavor and ease of preparation, always by the same team member, using the same equipment.

2 Next, another team member follows the recipe as written, **varying the brands of ingredients** and **kinds of equipment.** Even the types of stoves we use are changed.

3 A third team member repeats the whole process using **yet another set of equipment** and **alternative ingredients.**

By the time the recipes appear on these pages, they are guaranteed to work in any kitchen, including yours. We promise.

HEARST BOOKS
New York
An Imprint of Sterling Publishing
387 Park Avenue South
New York, NY 10016

ISBN 978-1-61837-173-7

Good Housekeeping

Rosemary Ellis	Editor in Chief
Courtney Murphy	Creative Director
Janet Siroto	Executive Editor
Susan Westmoreland	Food Director
Samantha B. Cassetty, MS, RD	Nutrition Director
Sharon Franke	Kitchen Appliances & Food Technology Director

Book design by Jon Chaiet
Project editor Sarah Scheffel
Photography credits on page 126.

Distributed in Canada by Sterling Publishing
c/o Canadian Manda Group, 165 Dufferin Street
Toronto, Ontario, Canada M6K 3H6

Distributed in the United Kingdom by GMC
Distribution Services
Castle Place, 166 High Street, Lewes, East Sussex,
England BN7 1XU

Distributed in Australia by Capricorn Link (Australia)
Pty. Ltd.
P.O. Box 704, Windsor, NSW 2756, Australia

www.goodhousekeeping.com

For information about custom editions, special sales, and premium and corporate purchases, please contact Sterling Special Sales at 800-805-5489 or specialsales@sterlingpublishing.com.

This special edition was printed for Kohl's Department Stores, Inc. (for distribution on behalf of Kohl's Cares, LLC, its wholly owned subsidiary) by Hearst Books, a division of Sterling Publishing.

KOHL'S
ISBN 978-1-61837-173-7
Factory Number: 123386
7/14

Manufactured in China

2 4 6 8 10 9 7 5 3 1

www.sterlingpublishing.com